CYBERPUNKS
CYBERFREEDOM
CHANGE REALITY SCREENS

by Timothy Leary

RONIN

Berkeley,

T012606+

Timothy Leary
Fugitive Philosopher
CyberPunk Time Traveler

CYBERPUNKS
CYBERFREEDOM
CHANGE REALITY SCREENS

by Timothy Leary

CyberPunks CyberFreedom
Change Reality Screens

Copyright 2008: The Futique Trust
ISBN: 978-1-57951-084-8

Published by
Ronin Publishing, Inc.
PO Box 22900
Oakland, CA 94609
www.roninpub.com

Production:

Editor:	Beverly A. Potter, Ph.D.
	docpotter.com
Cover Design:	Brian Groppe
	BrianGroppe.com
Book Design:	Beverly A. Potter

Fonts:

Big Cheese light and dark—Emigre
Century Schoolbook—Monotype
ITC Machine—Adobe Systems/Linotype
Univers—Adobe Systems

Library of Congress Card Number: 2008931384
Distributed to the book trade by **PGW/Perseus**
Printed in the United States by **Data Repro**

Derived from *Chaos & Cyber Culture.*

RONIN BOOKS FOR INDEPENDENT MINDS

by Timothy Leary

High Priest

Chaos & Cyber Culture

The Politics of Ecstasy

Psychedelic Prayers

Change Your Brain

The Politics of Self-Determination

Start Your Own Religion

Your Brain Is God

Turn On Tune In Drop Out

Musings on Human Metamorphoses

Evolutionary Agents

The Politics of PsychoPharmacology

The Fugitive Philosopher

Think for Yourself
Change Your Reality Screen

TABLE OF CONTENTS

You are only as old as the last time you changed your mind. I changed my mind often.

Reboot Your Brain!

1

THE ETERNAL PHILOSOPHY OF CHAOS

or several thousand years it has seemed obvious that the basic nature of the universe is extreme complexity, inexplicable disorder—that mysterious, tangled magnificence popularly known as Chaos. The poetic Hindus believed the universe was a dreamy dance of illusion that they called *maya*. The paradoxical, psychological Buddhists spoke of a void too complex—maybe a trillion times too complex—to be grasped by the human A-B-C-1-2-3 word-processing system—the mind.

Chinese poet-philosopher Lao-tzu sardonically reminded us that the *tao* is forever changing complexities at light speed, elusive and inaccessible to our fingers and thumbs laboriously tapping letters on our alphanumeric keyboards and mind-operating systems.

Individualistic thinking is the original sin of the Judo-Christian-Islamic Bibles. It sabotages attempts by the authorities to order Chaos.

> Law-and-order systems trivialize and demonize the dangerous concepts of Self—individual aims and personal knowledge. Thinking for Your Self is heretical, treasonous, blasphemous.

Socrates, that proud, self-reliant Athenian democrat, indiscreetly blurted out the dangerous secret when he said, *"The aim of human life is to know thy self."* This is surely the most subversive T-shirt flaunted over the centuries by humanists, the most confrontational bumper sticker on their neuro-auto-mobiles.

The first rule of every law-and-order system is to trivialize and demonize the dangerous concepts of Self—individual aims and personal knowledge. Thinking for Your Self is heretical, treasonous, blasphemous. Only devils and satans do it. Creative thinking, committed out loud, becomes a capital crime. It was "Three Strikes and You're Out" for several hundred thousand Protestant dissenters during the Inquisitions of the Roman papacy—not to forget the witch burnings performed by the Protestants when they took charge of the Chaos control department.

It was all very simple to the law-and-order controllers. There are the immortal Gods and Goddesses up there in that Gated Community on Olympus Drive. And then there are us—meaningless mortals, slaving around down here in the low-rent flatlands.

The concept of individuals with choice and identity seemed total folly, the ultimate nightmare—not just of authoritarian bureaucrats, but of common-sense liberals. Chaos must be controlled!

The standard way to tame and domesticate the impossible complexity that surrounds us is to invent a few "tooth-fairy" Gods, the more infantile the better, and to lay down a few childish rules: Honor your father and your mother, etc. The rules are simple and logical. You passively obey. You pray. You sacrifice. You work. You believe.

And then, Praise the Bored, let there be no terrorizing notions about individuals hanging around this meaningless, disordered universe trying to figure how to design themselves into individual selves.

Chaos Engineering

 The first Chaos engineers may have been the Hindu sages who designed a method for operating the brain called yoga. The Buddhists produced one of the great hands-on do-it-yourself manuals for operating the brain: *The Tibetan Book of the Dying*. Chinese Taoists developed the teaching of going with the flow—not clinging to idea-structures, but changing and evolving. The message was: Be cool. Don't panic. Chaos is good. Chaos creates infinite possibilities.

The wacko Socratic idea of Do It Yourself (D.I.Y.), which created modern democracy, was a

The first Chaos engineers may have been the Hindu sages who designed a method for operating the brain called yoga.

practical, common sense, sassy Athenian version of the Hindu Buddhist Taoist yogas. And remember where this foolishness got Tibet? Know-where!

The most dangerous idea is this crazed, megalomaniac Socratic notion of KNOW which defines the serf-human being as a thinker. Outrageous impudence! The slave is encouraged to become a philosopher! The serf strives to be a psychologist! A potential yogic sage!

This heresy predicts why later atheist evolutionists like Linnesus and Darwin defined our super chimp species as *Femina (Homo) sapiens*.

Chinese Taoists developed the teaching of going with the flow— not clinging to idea-structures, but changing and evolving. The message was: Be cool. Don't panic. Chaos is good. Chaos creates infinite possibilities.

The Chaos Without

For centuries there existed a fanatic taboo against scientific understanding. Why? Because of the fear of Chaos. The facts about our (apparently) insignificant place in the galactic dance are so insulting to the control freaks who try— so manfully and diligently and seriously—to manage Chaos that they forbade any intelligent attempts to look out there and dig the glorious complexity.

At one point consciousness altering devices like the microscope and telescope were criminalized for exactly the same reasons that psychedelic plants were banned in later times. They allow us to peer into bits and zones of Chaos.

Galileo got busted and Bruno got the Vatican microwave for showing that the Sun did not circle the Earth. Religious and political Chaosphobes naturally want the nice, tidy, comfy universe to cuddle around them.

In the last century science has developed technical extensions of the human sensorium that specify the truly spooky nature of the complexities we inhabit.

Stellar astronomy describes a universe of fantastic multiplicity: a hundred billion tiny star systems in our tiny galaxy, a hundred billion galaxies in our teeny universe.

The Chaos Within

 In the last decades of the 20th Century, scientists began to study the complexity within the human brain.

Talk about Chaos! It turns out that the brain is a galactic network of a hundred billion neurons. Each neuron is an information system as complex as a mainframe computer. Each neuron is connected to ten thousand other neurons. Each of us is equipped with a universe of neurocomplexity that is inscrutable to our alphanumeric minds.

This brain power is at once the most humiliating fact about our current ignorance, and the most thrilling prospect of our potential divinity—once we start learning how to operate our brain.

The Navigational Game Plan

Chaos theory allows us to appreciate our assignments: the understanding, enjoyment, and celebration of the delightful nature of the whole universe—including the totally mad paradoxes within our brains.

Activating the so-called right brain eliminates one of the last taboos against understanding Chaos and provides a hands-on scientific basis for the philosophy of humanism—encouraging us to team up with others to design our own personal versions of Chaos.

During the Roaring 20th Century, the equations for quantum physics led to the development of quantum appliances that allowed humans to receive, process, and transmit electronic images.

2

HOW I BECAME AN AMPHIBIAN

n 1980, Ronald Reagan, a screen person, became the president of the United States. At
the same time, the screen image of an Iranian
mullah, the leader of a notoriously irritable fundamentalist sect, became the rallying point of the
Islamic world. In the same year, surveys showed
that the average American spent more than four
hours a day neuronarcotized by the artificial
realities and fake news dramas on television
screens—more time than is spent on any other
waking activity in the flesh-material reality.

It was about then that I too found myself mutating gradually, imperceptibly, into an amphibi-
ous form. The word "amphibian" comes from the
Greek *amphi*—double, and *bios*—life.

I began spending around four hours a day
producing and scripting and directing the images on my personal screen. Some of these digitized words and images were my own. Some
were encoded on disks. Others were phoned to
me by friends and colleagues at almost the speed
of light.

In this way I learned how to file, process, organize, clarify, store, retrieve, and transmit my digitized thoughts in the form of words and icons.

These exercises in translating thoughts to digital codes and screen images have helped me understand how my brain works, how the universe evolves in terms of information algorithms. And, in the most practical mode, to understand:

1. How we can avoid television dictatorships, and

2. How we can democratize the cyberscreen politics of the future.

My experiences, far from being original or unique, seem to be part of an enormous cultural metamorphosis. Like millions of others, I came to feel as comfortable in Cyberia, Tubeland, on the other side of my electronic-reality window, as I do operating in the closed-in Terrarium of the material world. My brain, like yours, needs to be clothed in cyberwear and to swim, float, navigate through the oceans of electronic data.

Surely we can be forgiven if we are confused by all this. Organisms in the process of metamorphosis are forced to use the metaphors of past stages in order to anticipate future stages—an obviously risky business. "They'll never get me up in one of those," says the caterpillar to the butterfly.

"They'll never get me up in one of those," says the caterpillar to the butterfly.

From Aquaria to Terrarium to Cyberia

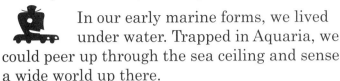In our early marine forms, we lived under water. Trapped in Aquaria, we could peer up through the sea ceiling and sense a wide world up there.

In the Devonian period—400 million years ago—we started developing the technology needed to migrate to the shoreline. I am talking state-of-the-art terra wear: skin-tight dry suits to maneuver around in the land world. Thus we became amphibians, able to live both in Aquaria and in Terrarium.

During the Thassic period we evolved to the mammalian stage and lost our ability to inhabit Aquaria. For the last 225 million years, we mammals crawled and ran around the Earth's surface, nervously improving our Terrarium survival technologies.

Then, during the last million or so years, human beings developed enormous brains that we did not know how to operate. Our hairless primate ancestors—banded in social groups, living in caves, fashioning clubs to fight tigers—were equipped with the same brain model that we are just now learning how to operate.

And for thousands of years, the more poetic or neurologically advanced among us have gazed upward on starry nights, beginning to realize that another universe exists in space and that we are trapped in the Terrarium of Earth's surface. Or what's a heaven for?

Around 1900, physicists like Einstein and Heisenberg demonstrated that the elements of all energy matter in the universe, out there or down here, consist of quanta of information. Light.

During the Roaring 20th Century, the equations of quantum physics led to the development of quantum appliances that allowed humans to receive, process, and transmit electronic images. Telephone, cinema, radio, television, computers, compact discs, fax machines; suddenly humans were creating digital realities that were accessed on living-room screens.

This universe of electronic signals, in which we now spend so much time, has been called Cyberia.

Just as the fish brain had to don dry-skin terra-suits to inhabit the Terrarium, and just as our primate brains had to don Canaveral space suits to explore outer space, our brains need cyberwear and digital appliances to inhabit cyberspace.

The Brain as a Digital Transmitter

As our brain evolves, it develops new vehicles and information-processing devices in order to feed its insatiable hunger for stimulation. Like any adolescent organ, the human brain requires an enormous, continual supply of chemical and electronic data to keep growing toward maturity.

In my last decade, the dendritic metabolism of my information organ—my brain—seems to have undergone a dramatic change. My eyes became two hungry mouths pressed against the Terrarium window through which electronic pulses reached the receptive areas of my brain. My brain seemed to require a daily input of several billion bytes of digital light speed information. In this I was no different from the average, televoid American sluggishly reclining on the bottom of the Terrarium. My brain also required regular diets of chemical foods. But my Very Personal Computer transformed my brain into an output organ emitting, discharging digital information through the Terrarium window into ScreenLand.

Just as my heart was programmed to pump blood, my sinewy brain was programmed to fire, launch, transmit, beam thoughts through the electronic window into Cyberia. The screen became the revolving glass door through which my brain both received and emited her signals.

As a result of personal computers and video arcades, millions of us are no longer satisfied to peer like passive infants through the Terrarium wall into the ScreenLand filled with cyber stars like Bill and Hillary and Boris and Obama and Paris Hilton and Beavis and Butt Head. We are learning how to enter and locomote in Cyberia. Our brains are learning how to exhale as well as inhale in the datasphere.

Of course, not all humans will make this move. Many of our finny ancestors preferred to remain marine forms. "You'll never get me up in one of those," said the tadpole to the frog.

Many humans will be trapped by gene-pool geography or compelled by repressive societies

or seduced by material rewards and thus re-
side in the material-flesh world of mammalian
bipeds. Oh, yeah. To escape from the boredom
and to rest alter their onerous, mech-flesh la-
bors, they will torpidly ingest electronic realities
oozing from their screens; but they will not don
cyber suits and zoom into ScreenLand.

We tri-brains who learn to construct and inhabit auto-realities spend some time in the cyber
world and some in the material-organic world.
We zoom through the datmosphere like Donkey
Kongs and Pac Woman, scooping up info-bits
and spraying out electronic-reality forms. And
then we cheerfully return to the slow, lascivious,
fleshy material world to indulge our bodies with
sensory stimulation and to exercise our muscles
by pushing around mechanical realities in sport
or recreation.

On the skin-tissue plane, our left brains are
limited to mechanical-material
forms. But in ScreenLand our
right brains are free to imagineer digital dreams, visions, fictions, concoctions, hallucinatory
adventures. All these screen
scenes are as real as a kick-in-
the-pants as far as our brains
are concerned. Our brains
have no sense organs and no
muscles. Our brains command
our bodies and send spaceships
to the Moon by sending signals
in only one linguistic: the quantum language of zeros and ones.

In ScreenLand our right brains are free to imagineer digital dreams, visions, fictions, concoctions, hallucinatory adventures.

No More Mind-Body Paradox

 We tri-brain creatures seem to be re-solving that most ancient philosophic problem. Forget the quaint, mammalian dualism of mind versus body. The interplay of life now involves digital brain-body matter-digital screen.

Everything—animal, vegetable, mineral, tangible, invisible, electric—is converted to digital food for the info-starved brain. And now, using the new digital appliances, everything that the brain mind can conceive can be realized in electronic patterns.

To be registered in consciousness, to be "realized," every sensory stimulation must be deconstructed, minimalized, digitalized. The brain converts every pressure signal from our skins, tickles from our genitals, delectables from our tongues, photons from our eyes, sound waves from our ears, and, best of all, electronic buzziness from our screens into quantum realities, into directories and files of 0/1 signals.

We tri-brain amphibians are learning how to use cyber wear—computer suits—to navigate around our ScreenLands the way we use the hardware of our bodies to navigate around the material-mechanical world, and the way we use spaceships and space suits to navigate around the outer space.

There are some amusing and alluring philosophic by-products. Quantum psychology allows us to define, operationally, other terms of classical metaphysics.

A Definition of "Spiritual" Could Be "Digital"

Recite to yourself some of the traditional attributes of the word "spiritual"—mythic, magical, ethereal, incorporeal, intangible, nonmaterial, disembodied, ideal, platonic. Is that not a definition of the electronic-digital?

Can We Engineer Our Souls?

Can we pilot our souls? The closest you are probably ever going to get to navigating your soul is when you are piloting your mind through your brain or its external simulation on cybernetic screens. Think of the screen as the cloud chamber on which you can track the vapor trail of your platonic, immaterial movements. If your digital footprints and spiritual fingerprints look less than soulful on the screen, well, just change them. Learning how to operate a soul figures to take time.

The quantum-electronic universe of information defines the new spiritual state. These "spiritual" realms, over centuries imagined, may, perhaps, now be realized! The more philosophic among us find this philosophically intoxicating.

Amphibians Will Not Neglect the Body

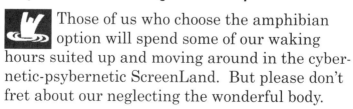 Those of us who choose the amphibian option will spend some of our waking hours suited up and moving around in the cybernetic-psybernetic ScreenLand. But please don't fret about our neglecting the wonderful body.

The first point to register is this: We tri-brains should not use our precious fleshware to work. Is it not a sacrilegious desecration to waste our precious sensory equipment on toil, chore, drudgery? We are not pack animals, or serfs, or executive robots garbed in uniforms rushing around lugging briefcases to offices. Why should we use our priceless, irreplaceable bodies to do work that can be done better by assembly-line machines?

But who will plough the fields and harvest the grapes? The languorous Midwestern farmer will done her cybersuit and while reclining in her hammock in Acapulco she will operate the automated plough on her Nebraska farm. The winemaker while reclining in his hammock on vacation in Acpulco will use his cybergear to direct the grape-crushing machines.

When we finish our work, we will take off our cybersuits, our brain clothing, and don body clothes. When we platonic migrants sweat, it will be in athletic or sensual pleasure. When we exert elbow grease, it will be in some form of painterly flourish or musical riff. When we operate oil gulping machines, we will joyride for pleasure. The only mechanical vehicles we will actually climb into and operate by hand will be sports cars. Trains, planes, boats will be used only for pleasure cruising, and will transport our bodies for athletic, artistic, recreational purposes only. Our bodily postures will thus be graceful and proud, our body movements delightful, slow, sensual, lush, erotic, fleshly, carnal vacations from the accelerated, jazzy cyber realities of cyberspace, where the brain work is done.

Personal Appearance in the Precious Flesh

Face-to-face interactions will be reserved for special, intimate, precious, sacramentalized events. Flesh encounters will be rare and thrilling. In the future each of us will be linked in thrilling cyber exchanges with many others whom we may never meet in person and who do not speak our phonetic literal language. Most of our important creations will take place in ScreenLand. Taking off our cyber wear to confront another with naked eyeballs will be a precious personal appearance. And the quality of our "personal appearances" will be raised to a level of mythic drama.

Common-Sense Quantum Psychology

 Before I acquired a personal computer, the principles of quantum physics always seemed, to my immature material mind, to be incomprehensible, bizarre, abstract, and totally impractical. After my digital brain lobes had been activated, quantum physics seems to make common sense and to define a practical psychology of everyday life in the tri-brain mode.

Einstein's theories of relativity, for example, suggest that realities depend on points of view. Instead of the static absolutes of space-time defined by material reality, quantum-brain realities are changing fields defined by quick feedback interchanges with other information sources. Our computer brainware allows us to perform Einsteinian-spiritual transformations on our laptops.

Werner Heisenberg's principle states that there is a limit to objective determinacy. If everyone has a singular viewpoint, constantly changing, then everyone creates his or her own version of reality. This gives the responsibility for reality construction not to a bad-natured biblical God, or to an impersonal, mechanical process of entropic devolution, or to an omniscient Marxist state, but to individual brains. Subjective determinacy operates in ScreenLand. Our brains create our own spiritual worlds, as they say along the Ganges. We get the realities we deserve. Or preserve. Or construct

And now our interactivated brains can project wonderland realities onto our screens and hurl them around the globe at light speed. Notice the political implications. Quantum psychology stressing singularity of viewpoint is the ultimate democratic perspective. The screen is the window to the new world. Who controls our screens programs the realities we inhabit. Therefore it behooves us to control our own reality screens.

These two notions, of relativity and self determination, are street smart common sense. But Einstein and Heisenberg and Max Planck and Niels Bohr lost the crowd when they said that the basic elements of the universe were bits of off/on yin/yang information. And that solid matter is temporary clusters of frozen information. And that when material structures are fissioned, they release energy: $E=mc^2$.

These brilliant physicists were explaining electronic

Learning how to operate a soul takes time.

The brain is an organ designed to metabolize digital information. ideas by using their hands to write with paleolithic chalk on a slab of black slate!

During the next twenty to eighty years, quantum appliances became household items. The application of quantum physics to engineering produced vacuum tubes, transistors, integrated circuits, lasers, radio, television, computers. These gadgets are not intended to move "matter energy" around. Instead, they move information. Data-buzzes. Electronic means "informational." Sticks and stones may break your bones, but information can never hurt you. Although it can, alas, totally control your mind.

So it becomes clear that the basic "particles" that make up matter are bits of "information." Matter is frozen information. Energy is just the dumb smoke and sweat that matter releases in its lumbering transformations. The famous formula changes to: $I=mc^2$, where *"I"=information*.

At the quantum level the Newtonian "laws" turn out to be local ordinances. It turns out that the smaller the linguistic element, the greater the I.Q.—Information Quotient. The larger is always the lumbering vehicle for the miniaturized, platonic info units it carries around. The universe is an intelligence system, and the elements of intelligence are quanta. And suddenly we understand that the brain is an organ designed to metabolize digital information.

Quantum Psychology in the Roaring 20th Century

Except to those who had studied the brilliantly intuitive metaphors of oriental philosophy, these principles of quantum psychology sounded implausible and weird when they were first announced around A.D. 1900. But looking back we can see that every decade of the Roaring 20th Century has produced events that have confirmed and applied quantum principles.

The philosophy of the 20th century, since Peirce and Saussure, is linguistic, semiotic, semantic. So is the psychology, and the politics. Modern art, modern writing, modern music made us feel comfortable in the quantum atmosphere. The great artists dissolved representational structure, freed elements to create new forms, word patterns, sounds, and accepted the responsibility of subjective reality-formation. As Walk Disney demonstrated, the brain loves to be electronized.

And now we have interpersonal computers, power gloves, CDs and DVDs, IPODS, social networking sites, electronic bulletin boards. All of these place the power to create platonic, electronic realities in the hands of interacting individuals.

Exploring the Brain

The advent of psychedelic—mind-opening—drugs in the Sixties produced a widespread fascination with consciousness alteration, mind exploration, inner searching, brain-stimulation gadgets, oriental yoga—all based on quantum principles. The advent of personal and interpersonal computers, digital editors, and audio-video gear at the end of the century turned the average American home into an electronic-information center. At the same time, neurologists were publishing their discoveries about how neurotransmitter chemicals and electrical nets move information around the brain.

The convergence of these waves of information, the inner psychedelic and the ScreenLand cybernetic, made it possible for the first time for human beings to understand how the brain operates. The human brain is, by auto definition, the most powerful control communication unit in the known universe. A constellation of a hundred billion cells floating in an ocean of info-gel. The brain has no muscles and no sense organs. It is a shimmering sea swarming with microchip molecules packaged in enormous hardware neurons, all linked by chemical-electrical signals. We could not understand how the brain operates until our electrical engineers built computers. And now we are learning how to beam our brain waves into the Cyberia of electronic reality, to think and play and work and communicate and create at this basic 0/1 level.

Our hundred-billion-neuron bio-computer brains are designed to process digital signals at the rate of a hundred fifty million per second.

Our hundred-billion-neuron computers are designed to process digital signals at the rate of a hundred fifty million per second. Each neuron can unfold as many as ten thousand dendrite receptors to pick up information from its neighbors. Talk about local-area networks! Talk about Central Intelligence Activity! More information is probably exchanged per second at the site of one synapse than in the CIA headquarters in a day. If any.

This is the reality field that Plato described in the 4th Century B.C., that quantum mechanics intuited in 1900, and that we tri-brains began to inhabit at the end of the Roaring 20th Century.

Power to the Singularities

The nature of the quantum politics of thought processing and the human-computer interaction was dramatically changed by the introduction and marketing of digital home appliances.

We can now create electronic realities on the other side of the screen not just with a keyboard or a joystick or a mouse. We wear the interface. We don cybergloves, cybergoggles, cybercaps, cybervests, cybershorts! Our bodily movements create the images on our screens. We walk, talk, dance, swim, float around in digital worlds, and we interact on screens with others who are linked in our nets.

Cyberwear is a mutational technology that allows individual's brains to experience OOB—out-of-body—experiences just as landware like legs and lungs permitted the fish to escape the water— OOW experiences. Cyberwear will make it possible for individual Americans to cross the Merlin Wall and to meet and interact in cyberspace.

Pioneers of Cyberspace

The basic notion of OOB artificial-reality appliances was introduced by Myron Kreuger and Ted
Nelson in the 1970s. The nitty-gritty realities of
creating and inhabiting digital universes were
described in 1985 by William Gibson in his brilliant, epic trilogy *Neuromancer Count Zero*, and
Mona Lisa Overdrive. Gibson described the "ma-
trix," the dataworlds created by human digital
communication. By 1989 cybernauts like Jaron
Lanier, Eric Gullichsen, Joi Ito, Brenda Laurel,
and Rebecca Allen were developing cyberspace
realities built for two. Or more.

Realities Built for Two

Many people are understandably disturbed by
the idea that in the future human beings will be
spending more time in ScreenLand than in Flesh
Play; piloting their brain-selves inside electronic
realities, interacting with other electronic humans.

Like adolescents whose hormones suddenly
awaken the unused sexual circuits of their brains,
we tri-brains are just now discovering that the brain
is an info-organ wired, fired, and inspired to process
and emit electronic signals. The main function of a
computer is interpersonal communication.

Soon many of us will be spending almost all our
screen time actively zooming around digital oceans
interacting and recreating with other tri-brains.

Some industrial-age cynics say that humans
are too lazy. They would rather sit back as sed-
entary couch slugs than be active. But we've
been through these tech-jumps before in history.

Before Henry Ford, only big shot engineers and captains employed by corporations drove mass-media vehicles such as trains and steamboats. Now we recognize—and often deplore—this genetic compulsion to grab the steering wheel, smoke rubber, and freely auto mobilize that sweeps over every member of our species at puberty.

Soon most of our daily operations—occupational, educational, recreational—will transpire in ScreenLands. Common sense suggests that we are more likely to find compatible brainmates if we are not restricted to local geography or to physical bodies.

Cyberwear will make it possible for individual Americans to cross the Merlin Wall and to meet and interact in cyberspace.

3

CUSTOM-SIZED SCREEN REALITIES

For thousands of years, since the dawn of tribal societies, most human beings have lived in drab caves, huts, shacks, igloos, houses, or apartments furnished and supplied with minimum information equipment-oral-body language. Stone tools.

In these shut-in, introverted, inward-looking, data-starved abodes occurred the practical maintenance time-dons that people had to perform to keep the gene pool going. For most people the plumbing was crude, the clothing hardly seductive. Cosmetics and perfumes were minimal—to say the most.

In the tribal culture there were no books, radios, or daily newspapers. No *Vogue* magazine loaded with five hundreds slick pages of silk fashion, voluptuous models pouting with desire, straining to arouse, flashing wide-open, inviting legs in high-heeled shoes, and curving, suck-me tits. No, the survival information needed to maintain the tribal home was packaged in rote, monkey-like signals expressed by the body: oral grunts, gestures, bodily movements, crude artifacts.

The Tribal-Culture Show

If we wanted to experience a bit of glamour, if we yearned to flirt around, looking for a sexual partner, or to check on what was happening, if we needed a battery recharge to keep us going as a loyal gene-pool serf-servant, we had to exit the home and amble up to the village square. There we could get the evening tribal news, pick up the local gossip, and make deals for skins or fur coats for our wives in exchange for a stone knife.

On designated occasions, our entire tribe would swarm together for ceremonies of celebration: Planting. Harvesting. Full moons. Solstice flings. Weddings. Funeral orgies. In agricultural societies the ingestion of psychotropic vegetables has always provided the sacramental energy for the gene-pool gatherings. Wines, fermented grains, brain change vines, roots, leaves, flowers containing the precious neurotransmitters prepared and administered by alchemical shamans produced the "high," the venerable, sacred, precious transcendental state of chaotics, ecstasy, possession, revelation, trance—the mythic-genetic right-brain vision. The Holy Confusion.

You know what I'm talking about. What orgasm is to the body, this shuddering psychedelic experience is to the brain.

At these treasured high moments, we tribe members could escape the drab and activate our individual myths, our special inner talents, and we could communicate it to others who were navigating their own personal neurorealities.

These intense communications, brain exchanges which Catholics call "Holy Communion," we call the Holy Confusion. At these ceremonies we tribe members could express our visions in communal theatre. This one becomes a jokester. Another sings. Another dances. Suddenly tricksters, artists, mimes take the center stage to act out the emotions and the identifying themes that held the tribe together.

Sponsors of the tribal show time?

The clique that ran the tribe. The priests and the chieftains. The lovable grey beards, the stern, traditional Old Ones. The studio heads. Those responsible for holding the tribe together for their own fame and profit

The task of luring the populace to listen to the sponsors' messages in the feudal-industrial ages was delegated to a special caste called: The talent. The painters. The directors. The shaman. The architects. The entertainers. The minstrels. The storytellers. Their function and duty in the tribal economy was to calm the fears of Chaos with delightful comforting fantasies, titillating ceremonies, and romantic dramas.

We could let our swollen, tumescent eyeballs pop wide open and our turgid, drooling peasant tongues dangle as we watched the belly dancers and muscular dudes wiggle, writhe, slither, jiggle, and quiver until our loins ached. When we were back in the

What orgasm is to the body, this shuddering psychedelic experience is to the brain.

dark cave/hut in fireplace flicker, our plain, glam-
ourless, loyal mates suddenly turned into the
Whores of Babylon! Krishnas with glowing hard-
ons! Talk about pornography inciting desire!

The perennial problem with the directors and
the talent is this. To attract and dazzle villagers
to listen to the commercials, they had to allow
the public to vicariously experience this steamy,
smoking hot, exciting, naughty stuff that was
absolutely taboo for the people, but which could
be acted out in morality plays, racy festival
performances, sculptures of naked bodies. And
here's where we talents come in.

To keep the folks tuning in, the sponsors needed us performers. The sexy musicians, well-en-
dowed dancers, clowns, raunchy comedians telling risque stories about adulteries and risky new
sexual adventures, poets, X-rated storytellers,
comics, mimes. It was the talent who performed
the safety-valve function, who gave the populace
a fantasy taste of the rich and forbidden fruits.

Talents were selected for beauty, erotic
charm, powerful emotion. We were expected to
go too far, to push the envelope of taboo, to test
the limits of good taste. Show our tits and asses.
Act out wild copulatory sex dances. Scandalize.
And we were required to suffer the consequenc-
es. We were banned. Blacklisted. Sold down the
river. Forced into harlotry. Fired from Harvard.
Forever shamed and exposed in the local version
of the perennial *National Enquirer*. Denounced
as devils from the pulpits of the orthodox
preachers, and denounced as C.I.A. agents by
Marxists.

The sponsors of the tribal show, the priests and the chiefs, were kept busy not only producing the event, but also watching and censoring and punishing to make sure that nothing got too far out of hand, or upset the sponsors. And, of course, the gene-pools commercials were ever-present. We could never forget who owned the drums and the rattles and the spears and the shamanic talent, and the temples. The patrons who paid for the tribal show.

4

THANK GOD FOR FEUDALISM

Marshall **McLuhan** spoke wisely. "Change the media and you change the culture." Literacy upgraded the aesthetic level and the efficiency of the entertainment packaging. The growth of cities and nations by the 1st Century B.C. provided big budgets and big crews to distribute continual messages from the gene-pool sponsors.

The people, the average folk, the sixpack-Joe families, were now called plebes or serfs or peasants. Their role in the feudal-information economy was not that different from that of their tribal ancestors. The poor people are always seen as primitive because they are forced to live in tribal neighborhoods, ghettos, in huts, shacks, windowless rooms, slum pads, shabby urban caves where the signal rate was limited to immediate biological data exchanges from first breath to death.

The cultural and political messages from the sponsors of the feudal age were popularized and disseminated in spectacular public broadcasts. The church in the central plaza was large, ornate, decorative, loaded with statues and paintings of truly inspired aesthetic genius. The mediaeval crime time show, both Christian and Islamic, was performed by miraculously gifted talent. The tiled mysteries of the Alhambra and the ceilings of the Vatican Chapel still inspire the breathless reflex reaction, "Wow! Praise the Lord for sponsoring this great show!"

Every day the commercial logos and mottoes of the feudal culture were repeated. The muezzin's call, the church bell's sonorous clang, the chanting of the monks, the colorful garb of the priests and mullahs. Stained glass!

No wonder these feudal religions—fundamentalist, fanatic, furious, passionate, paranoid—swept the Hooper ratings! The fellaheen could leave their scruffy hovels and walk through cathedrals with golden ceilings stretching to the sky, while candles flickered on the statues of the Prophet. A panoramic mosque-church scene throbbing with color, pomp, grandeur, wealth, and melodrama pouring into virginal eyeballs.

The palaces of the secular rulers, the kings and dukes, were equally stunning, and much more sexy. The priests may have preached sexual abstinence, but the nobles forked anyone they wanted to and celebrated sexual beauty in the paintings they commissioned. The walls of the palaces glowed with flamboyant celebrations of naked wantonness. Greek

The walls of the palaces glowed with flamboyant celebrations of naked wantonness.

goddesses with pink, swollen thighs and acres of soft, silky flesh sprawled on clouds of filmy desire, enticing their male counterparts to enjoy their favors.

You could stand humbly with cap in hand and cheer the swells dressed up in opulent lace and leather riding by in gold-decorated carriages. You loved the changing of the Guard, probably not realizing that the troops were there to protect the sponsors of the show from you, the people.

The shack you live in may be dreary, but ankle downtown to catch the big, spectacular God-King show.

Change the media

and you change the culture.

—Marshall McLuhan

5

THANK GUTENBERG-NEWTON FOR THE INDUSTRIAL AGE

T he same McLuhan trends continued in the industrial age. As usual, the populace was housed in small, dark rooms, but now that big is better, the rooms were stacked in enormous slum buildings.

The factory culture created the highest form of intelligent life on this planet, up until now: the mass-market consumer.

The sponsors of the factory economy didn't really plan to create an insatiable consumer class that would eventually overwhelm it with acquisitive desire. Quite the contrary. The sponsors of the industrial culture were those who belonged to the one class that easily survived the fall of feudalism: the engineer-managers. They were sometimes called Masons. They were white, anti-papist, Northern European mechanics, efficient and rational, with a scary hive mentality totally loyal to The Order. Stem puritans. They worked so hard, postponed so much pleasure, and got obsessed with engineering so efficiently that they ended up flooding the world with an unstoppable cascade of highly appealing products. Labor saving devices. Better medicines to save lives. Better guns to snuff lives. Books. Radios. Televisions.

This cornucopian assembly line of everything that a tribal hunter or a feudal serf or a Holy Roman Emperor could possibly have lusted for required endless rotating armies of indefatigably industrious consumers willing to lift items from shelves, haul grocery carts, unpack bags, store in refrigerators, kick tires, read manuals of instruction, turn keys, drive away, and then religiously repair, until death, the appliances that rolled like an endless river of metal-rubber-plastic down Interstate 101 to the shopping malls and into our factory-made homes.

How can the sponsors keep the people motivated to perform the onerous tasks of producing and consuming at a feverish pace? The same old way—by putting on a show and promising them a glimpse of the high life. But this time, in the mercantile culture, they can sell 'em tickets.

The cultural celebrations that got people out of the house in the industrial society were no longer religious-political ceremonies. They occurred in commercial venues. Public invited. Tickets at box office or street corner. Every community boasted a theatre, concert hail, art gallery, opera house, burlesque pal-

The factory culture created the highest form of intelligent life on this planet, up until now: The Mass-Market Consumer.

ace, vaudeville show, sports stadium, bullring. Etcetera. These entertainment factories were built to resemble the royal structures of the feudal age. Theatres were called the "Palace" and the "Majestic" and the "Royal."

In these plastic-fantastic whorehouse temples, workers could escape the routine, drab signalry of the workday and lose themselves in lascivious, wet-dream, hypnotic states of erotic pleasure, tantalizing, carnal carnivals designed and produced by us, the shamanic profession, the counterculture entertainers.

The psycho-economics were clear-cut. The consumers wanted the show to last as long as possible, anything to get out of the hovel. More was better. The show-biz trick was to stretch out the scenes of the opera, stage play, concert as long as possible. Give 'em their money's worth.

Films Present Electric Realities

 By the mid-20th Century, at the peak of the mechanical age, the relentless engineering search for labor saving devices and mass distribution naturally extended to the entertainment industry. The new McLuhan media was electricity. Stage plays could be filmed, the films duplicated and sent to hundreds of theatres.

The effect was astounding. Farmer Brown could sit in the village theatre and there in front of him, thirty-feet high, was the face of Clara Bow, her bulging red lips glistening with moisture, her eyes beaming nymphomaniac invitation! Farmer Brown had never in his wildest fantasies dreamed of this sultry thang! Meanwhile, Mrs. Brown is breathing Hard and leaking her precious bodily juices watching Rudolf Valentino licking his full lips with his sensual tongue

What Industrial Minds Want

Movies swept the world. The film industry naturally followed the commandment of the mechanical age—bigger is better. Cloned quantity is better. Feature films were made in two convenient sizes. The epic was very long. But the industry was run by clothing merchants from New York who knew how to sell, cut-rate, two pants to a suit. So most films were manufactured in the half size "double-bill." If and when the people left their homes and traveled downtown to the theatre, they expected a good three or four hours of escape.

Over the last twenty-five thousand years, until yesterday, the sponsors had come and gone, and the technologies had improved from oral-gestural to hand-tool to mechanical-electric. But the goals, principles, and venues of human motivation and human communication hadn't really changed much, and the economics hadn't changed. Big was always better.

The talent in tribal, feudal, and industrial cultures had two "charm" tasks. The first, and most important, was to entice, beg, grovel, seduce, use our sexual wiles, go down on our knees to the sponsors to get the deal. The second job was to please the customers. This was easier, because the customers basically were begging to get titillated, turned on, aroused. They had paid money to adore the talent.

The sponsors, of course, got their kicks from flicking over everyone, especially the glamorous talent. When and if the entertainers became superstars, they, naturally, got off their knees, wiped off their mouths, and proceeded to take exquisite revenge on the sleazy producers, the grubby studio heads, the rodent-like agency executives, the greedy managers, and the assorted lawyer thieves with briefcases and fax machines who had formerly abused us.

"There's no business like show business!" As they were fond of saying.

Learn How to Change the Screens

These ancient rituals, which endured through the tribal, feudal, industrial ages, amazingly enough, began to change dramatically in the last few years! Just before yesterday, around 1984, a combination of American creativity and Japanese precision suddenly mass-produced inexpensive, do-it-yourself home appliances for individuals to electronify, digitize, and transmit personal realities.

Digital communication translates the recording of any sound or photograph of any image into clusters of quanta or fuzzy clouds of off/on information. Any image digitized by an individual human can then be flashed on telephone lines around the world inexpensively at light speed.

Bigger is No Longer Better

The basic elements of the youniverse, according to quantum-digital physics, can be understood as consisting of quanta of information, bits of compressed digital programs, These elements of pure (0/1) information contain incredibly detailed algorithms to program potential sequences for fifteen billion years—and still running. These information-jammed units have only one hardware external function. All they do is flash off/on when the immediate environment triggers a complex array of "if if if if ... THEN!" algorithms.

Digital communication (i.e., the operation of the universe) involves massive arrays of these info units, trillions of information pixels flashing to create the momentary hardware reality of one single molecule.

The Newtonian energy- matter equations of the industrial age—the 19th Century—defined a local mechanical reality in

In the information age when packaging digital data, much smaller is very much better.

which much bigger and more was very much better. You remember the catch-phrases in the old Newtonian heavy metal Dinosaur Marching Song? Force. Momentum. Mass. Energy. Work. Power. Thermodynamics.

In the information age we are coming to realize that in packaging digital data, much smaller is very much better.

The basic principle in light-speed communication is that so much more information is packed into so much smaller hardware units. For example, the 2-pound human brain is a digital organic computer that processes a hundred million times more information (r.p.m.) than the 200-pound body.

The almost invisible DNA code keeps programming and constructing improved organic computing appliances, i.e., generation after generation of better and more portable brains. A billion-year-old DNA megaprogram of invisible molecular size is much smarter than the shudderingly fragile, here-and-now brain!

And infinitely smaller. People are learning to deal with enormous stacks of digital-electronic information presented at light speeds. Telephone. Radio. Television. Computers. Compact discs. At home. In their "head" quarters. Electronic info is pulled down from the sky and poured out of the portable stereophonic ghettoblaster perched on shoulder, jacked into ear-balls as the body dances along the avenue. This "addiction" to electronic information has drastically expanded the reception scope and lessened the tar pit attention span of the 19th Century.

Cybernetic Brains Expect More Data In Less Time

Folks in the mechanical age may be content to sit drinking tea and reading the *London Times* for two hours. But energetic smart people navigating a postindustrial brain move through an ocean of information, surfing data waves breaking at light speed.

This appetite for digital data, more and faster, can now be recognized as a species need.

The brain needs electrons and psychoactive chemicals like the body needs oxygen. Just as body nutritionists list our daily requirements for vitamins, so will our brain-psyberneticians soon be listing our daily requirements for various classes of digital information.

Soon pure information will be cheaper than water and electricity. The average American home will be equipped to access trillions of bits of information per minute. The credit-card-size interpersonal computer will be able to scoop up any page from the Library of Congress, sift through the entire film library of MGM, sort through all the episodes of "I Love Lucy," and slice out—if it pleases you—paragraphs from the original Aramaic Bible.

On a typical Saturday way back in 1990, Los Angeles residents with a competitive itch could exercise the option to flick on seven major-league baseball games, nine college football contests, the Olympic games, two horse-racing tracks, etc.

Soon even the poorest kid in the inner city will have a thumbnail-size chip—costing a dollar—with the storage and processing power of a billion transistors. He/she will also have an optic-fiber wall socket that will input a million times more signals than the current television set. Inexpensive virtual-reality suits and goggles will allow this youngster to interact with people all over the world in any environment he or she chooses to fabricate

As George Gilder says, "The cultural limitations of television, tolerable when there was no alternative, are unendurable in the face of the new computer technologies now on the horizon-technologies in which the U.S. leads the world."

The smart home, thus equipped with inexpensive digital appliances, becomes our private television film-sound studio that programs the digital universe we choose to inhabit, for as long as we want to inhabit it.

But is there not a danger of overload? The ability to scan and fish-net miniaturized, abridged, slippery bursts of essence aesthetic information from the salty oceans of signals flooding the home becomes a basic survival skill in the 21st Century. Our bored brains love "overload." They can process more than a hundred million signals a second.

Of course, this acceleration and compression of information has already become state of the art in television. The aim of crime-time network television is to get people to watch commercials. A 30-second slot during the Super Bowl broadcast costs more than a million dollars.

The advertising agencies were the first to pick up the handy knack of digital-miniaturization. They spurt dozens of erotic, shocking, eye-catching images into a half-minute info-slot convincing us that "the night belongs to Michelob." For that matter, we select our presidents and ruling bureaucrats on the basis of 30-second image clips, carefully edited by advertising experts.

Bigger is Not Better—Even in Movies

Slowly, reluctantly, the factory-based film industry is being forced to condense, speed up. Veteran, old -y are trapped in the antiquated industrial-age models of the opera and the "legitimate" stage play and the epic movie. And the prima-donna omnipotent director.

Before 1976, the bigger the movie the better. The long, leisurely, time-consuming film was the great epic. A director who came into the screening room with anything less than 2 hours—120 minutes or 7200 seconds—was considered a breezy lightweight.

Way back in 1966, before cable television, people loved long, slow films. They provided folks with a welcome escape from their info-impoverished homes. You went to the theatre to enter a world of technicoloured glamour and excitement that could not be experienced at convenience in the living room. In the theatre you could be Queen for a Night. The director, naturally enough, tried to stretch out the show as long as possible to postpone the customer's return to the home dimly lit by three black-and-white television networks.

This appetite for digital data, more and faster, can now be recognized as a species need.

Miniaturization

By the beginning of the century, however, most American residences were equipped with cable inputs and DVDs and remote controls, with flat screen TV coming in fast. Sitting like sultans in botanical torpor, we browse, graze, nibble as many multitone, flashing screen-fix as our warm little fingers can punch buttons.

We are no longer sensation-starved serfs pining in dark garrets, lusting, longing, craving, starved for the technicolour flash of soft curving flesh. On late night television we can bathe in sexual innuendo. We can rent X-rated films of every erotic version and perversion ever dreamed. There is no longer that desperate appetite, that starved hunger, that yearning itch, that raw hankering for optical stimulation.

For this reason the long, slow, symphony-scored feature film has become a plodding line of 150 elephants trapped in the melodramatic swamp. Movies today are far too long. The information-age cyber-person simply will not

We are no longer sensation-starved serfs.

sit for 150 minutes trapped in Cimino's wonderfully operatic mind or Coppolla's epic intensities. For many of us, the best stuff we see on a movie screen are the trailers. A new art form is emerging—the production of 3-minute teasers about coming attractions. Electronic haikus! Most movies fail to live up to the trailers that hype them. The "high lights" of a smash-grab action flick can be fascinating for 3 minutes, but lethally boring for 2 hours. Indeed, most of the new breed of movie directors learned their craft by making commercials or MTV clips, from which have come the new communication rhythms.

The brain needs electrons and psychoactive chemicals like the body needs oxygen. Just as body nutritionists list our daily requirements for vitamins, so will our brain-psyberneticians soon be listing our daily requirements for various classes of digital information.

Filmmakers are learning the lesson of quantum physics and digital neurology: much more data in much smaller packages. It turns out that the brain likes to have digital signals jamming the synapses.

Custom-Sized Movies

In response to this obvious fact, some innovative filmmakers are beginning to experiment with customized movies, sized for length. The idea is this. If you go to a good restaurant, you don't want to sit trapped at a table for 150 minutes eating the same Italian dish. No matter how delicious. No matter how many Oscars the chef has won, most younger film buffs are not gonna sit still during a 2 1/2-hour spaghetti film by moody, self-absorbed auteur-directors from the operatic traditions.

But if long, slow flicks are what you want, if you really prefer to absorb electronic information like a python ingests a pig, if you want to stuff yourself and slowly digest a 150-minute film—why, no problem! You arrive at the cineplex and you make your menu selection when you buy your ticket. If you want the super-giant 150-minute version of *Last Temptation of Christ* you pay $20, visit the rest room, pack a lunch, cancel a few meetings, walk to the long-distance room, settle in, and let Scorcese leisurely paddle you down his cerebral canals. As a television person, your

The brain likes to have digital signals jamming the synapses.

attention appetite at the visual banquet table probably gets satiated after an hour. So you'll tend to select the regular-size epic: Christ, $10 for 50 minutes.

But cyberplots and brain jocks, with an eternity of digitized info-worlds at fingertip, tend to go for the nouvelle cuisine, gourmet buffet. You pay $5 and watch five 10-minute "best-of," haiku compressions of five films. Five "high lights" essence-teasers. Tastes great! Less filling!

If you are really taken by one of these *specialite de maison* and want more, you either go to the box office for a ticket or you stick your credit card in the dispenser cabinet, dial your choice, and out pops a custom sized rental video to take home and scan at your convenience.

Do-It-Yourself Cyberware
Offers Personal Electronic Realities

So far you have been a busy consumer with many passive selective options. But suppose you want to move into the active mode? Change the film? Script and direct your own version? Put your personal spin on the great director's viewpoint. Heresy!

Suppose, for example, that you're a 14-year-old African or Asian girl and you dislike the movie *Rambo*, which cost $40 million, minimum to make. You rent the video for $2 and scan it. Then you select the most offensive section. Maybe the one where Sly Stallone comes crashing through the jungle into the native village, naked to the waist, brandishing a machine gun with which he kills several hundred Asian men, women and children.

To present your version, you digitize this 30-second scene, copy it into your $100 Nin-Sega-Mac computer, and use the Director software program to re-edit. You digitize the torso of a stupid-looking gorilla, you can a wilted celery stalk or the limp penis of an elephant, you loop in the voice of Minnie Mouse in the helium mode screaming the Stallone lines: "You gonna let us win this time?"

You pass your version into the rented tape, pop it back in the box and return it to the video store. The next person renting *Rambo* will be in for a laugh and a half! Within weeks this sort of viral contagion of individual choice could sweep your town.

In the cybernetic age now dawning, "Digital Power to the People" provides everyone this inexpensive option to cast, script, direct, produce, and distribute his or her own movie. Custom-made, tallorized, in the convenient sizes—mammoth, giant, regular, and byte-sized mini.

Energetic smart people navigating a postindustrial brain move through an ocean of information, surfing data waves breaking at light speed.

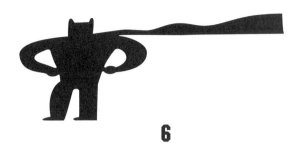

6

IMAGINEERING

I remember viewing a videotape filmed by cyberspace researchers at Autodesk, a Sausalito computer-software company. On the screen, a woman wearing tennis shorts leans ahead expecting a serve. On her head she wears a cap woven with thin wires. Her eyes are covered by opaque goggles. In her hand she holds a metal tennis racquet with no strings.

She dashes to her left and swings furiously at the empty air. "Oh no!" she groans in disappointment. "Too low!"

She crouches again in readiness then runs forward, leaps up, slams a vicious volley at the empty air and shouts in triumph.

The videotape then changes point of view. Now I am seeing what the player sees. I am in the court. The ball hits the wall and bounces back to my left. My racquet smashes the ball in a low-angle winning shot.

This woman is playing virtual racquet ball. Her goggles are two small computer screens

Does this sound too Star Trekky to be for real? Well, it's already happening.

showing the digitized three-dimensional picture of a racquetball court. She is in the court. As she moves her head-left, right, up-orientation-direction sensors in her cap show her the left wall, the right wall, the ceiling. The movement of the ball is calculated to reflect "real-life" gravity and spin.

I am experiencing the current big trend in electronics. It is called artificial reality or virtual reality or electronic reality. Some literary computer folks call it platonic reality, in honor of the Socratic philosopher who described a universe of idealized or imagined forms more than two thousand years ago. Cynics call it virtual banality.

We no longer need to press our addicted optical nostrils to the television screen like grateful amoebas. Now, we can don cybersuits, clip on cybergoggles, and move around in the electronic reality on the other side of the screen. Working, playing, creating, exploring with basic particles of reality-electrons.

This technology was first developed by NASA. The idea was that technicians in Houston could use their gloves to direct robots on the moon. Architects and engineers are experimenting with an Autodesk device to walk around in the electronic projections of the buildings they are designing. Doctors can travel down arteries and veins, observing and manipulating instruments.

Does this sound too Star Trekky to be for real? Well, it's already happening. Way back at Christmas 1990 six hundred thousand American kids equipped with Nintendo power gloves were sticking their hands through the Alice Window moving ninja warriors around.

The implications of this electronic technology for work and leisure and interpersonal intimacy are staggering.

For example, within a few years many of us will not have to "go" to work. We will get up in the morning, shower, dress in our cyberwear suits, and "beam" our brains to work. No more will we have to fight traffic in our air-polluting 300-horsepower cars, hunt for parking spaces, take the elevator to our offices. No more flying, strapped in our seats in a monstrous toxic-waste-producing air-polluting jet-propelled sky-dinosaur, jammed with sneezing, coughing sardines, fighting jet lag to attend conferences and meetings.

Tomorrow Our Brains Will Soar

Tomorrow our brains will soar on the wings of electrons into the offices of friends in Tokyo, then beam at light speed to a restaurant in Paris for a flirtatious lunch, pay a quick, ten-minute visit to our folks in Seattle—all without physically leaving our living rooms. In three hours of electronic, global house calls we can accomplish what would have taken three days or three weeks of lugging our brain-carrying bodies like slabs of inert flesh.

This is the information age, and the genera-tor-producers of information are our delightful, surprise-packed brains. Just as the enormously

We will get up in the morning, shower, dress in our cyberwear suits, and "beam" our brains to work.

powerful machines of the industrial age moved our bodies around, so, tomor-row, will our cybernetic appliances zoom our brains around the world at light speed.

We won't travel to play. We press two buttons and we are standing on the tee of the first hole at Pebble Beach. There to join us is sister Anita—who is actually standing on the lawn of her house in Atlanta—and our dear-est, funniest, wonderful friend Joi, whom we have never met in the flesh—and who is actually standing in his backyard in Osaka. Each of us in turn "hits" the platonic golf ball and we watch them soar down the fairway. After finishing the first hole, we can dial-beam to Anita's patio to admire her garden, zap over to the tee of the second hole at St. Andrew's, then zoom to the Louvre to look at that Cezanne painting Joi was talking about.

Most of us Americans spend half our wak-ing hours zapping around in electronic environ-ments with our friends. Any spot in the world we can think of can be dialed up on our screens with our friends. Any landscape, surrounding, setting, habitat we can think of or imagine can be quick-ly fabricated on our screens with our friends.

Some thoughtful critics are concerned by the prospect of human beings spending so much time trapped like zombies in the inorganic, plastic-fantastic electronic world. They fear that this will lead to a depersonalization, a dehuman-ization, a robotization of human nature, a race of screen-addicted nerds. This understandable apprehension is grounded in the horrid fact that today the average American spends around six hours each day passively reclining in front of the boob tube, and three hours a day peering docile-ly into Big Brother's computer screens.

The optimistic human scenario for the future involves three common-sense steps.

1. Cure the current apathetic, torpid tele-vision addiction.

2. End the monopoly of top-down, spud-farm, mass-media centralized televi-sion, and

3. Empower individuals to actively com-municate, perform, create electronic realities.

How? By means of inexpensive computer clothing.

Another example? A married couple, Tom and Jane, are walking down the Malibu beach. In material form, you understand. Real foot-massaging sand. Real skin-tanning sunshine blue sky. On loving impulse, they decide to spend a funny, loving minute or two with their daughter, Annie, who is in Boulder.

They flip down their lens-goggles that look like sunglasses. Jane punches a few numbers her stylish, designer wristwatch. Tom turns on the one pound Walkman receiver transmitter, In Boulder, Annie accepts their "visit" and dials them to a prefabricated pix scene of her patio. She is smiling in welcome. She is actually in her living room, but electrically she is in her electronic patio. They see exactly what they would see if they were there. When they turn their heads, they see Annie's husband Joe walking out waving. He points out the roses I have just bloomed in the garden. Remember, at the same time Tom and Jane are "really" walking down the Malibu beach. They can look over the goggles and watch two kids in bathing suits chasing a dog.

Reality designing is a team sport.

The four people sharing the "patio" reality decide they want to be joined by sister Sue, in Toronto. They dial her and she beams over to the "patio" in Colorado. Sue wants to show them her new dress; so the gang beams up to Sue's living room.

What'll It Cost?

It is logical for you, at this point, to wonder about the cost of transcontinental home movie-making. Is this not another expensive toy for affluent yuppies playing while the rest of the world starves?

Happily, the answer is "no." The equipment used by this family costs less than a standard television set, that pathetic junk-food spud-box with no power to store or process electronic information. Designing and digitizing and communicating the electronic realities costs less than a phone call. In ten years fiber-optic wires will receive transmit more information than all the clumsy air-wave broadcasting networks. A thumbnail size brain chip holding a billion transistors will allow us to store and process millions of three dimensional signals per minute. Intense chaotics waiting to be re-created.

What will we possibly do with these inexpensive extensions of our brains? The answer is so down to earth human. We shall use these wizard powers to communicate with each other at unimaginable levels of clarity, richness, and intimacy. Reality designing is a team sport.

Consider Erotic Interaction

To help us imagine one dimension of the communication possibilities, let us consider the erotic interaction. Cyril Connolly once wrote, "Complete physical union between two people is the rarest sensation which life can provide—and yet not quite real, for it stops when the telephone rings."

Connolly's comment is useful because he distinguishes between "physical" communication, bodies rubbing, and neurological signals—words and thoughts transmitted electrically. The solution to his problem is simple. Electronic appliances are beautifully cooperative. (Hey, Cyril, if you don't want to be disturbed, just turn the gadget off when you head for the sack, and then turn it back on when you wish to.)

But let us examine a more profound implication. Connolly refers to "complete physical union" as "the rarest sensation which life can provide." Is he thereby denigrating the "union of minds and brains"? The interplay of empathy, wit, fantasy, dream, whimsy, imagination? Is he scorning "platonic love"? Is he implying that sex should be mindless genital acrobatics? A grim, single-minded coupling that can be disturbed by the platonic rapture of metaphysical sex? Or a phone call?

Here is a typical episode of erotic play that could happen the day after tomorrow. The two lovers, Terry and Jerry, are performing bodily intercourse beautifully with elegance and sensual skill, etc. They are also wearing platonic lenses. At one point Jerry touches her/his watch, and suddenly they are bodysurfing twelve-foot rainbow waves that are timed to their physical erotic moves. Sounds of liquid magnificence flood their ears. Terry giggles and touches her/his watch, and the waves spiral into a tunnel vortex down which they spin and tumble. They intercreate reality dances. Terry is a seething volcano over whom Jerry soars as a fearless eagle, while birds sing and the Earth stiffly breathes.

Plato, it turns out, was magnificently on beam. He said that the material, physical expressions are pale, crude distortions of the idea forms that are fabricated by the mind, the brain, the "soul." We are talking about learning how to operate our minds, our brains, our souls. And learning the rudiments of mind-fucking, silky body juicy fucking, and brain-soul fucking.

In fact, most physical sex, even the most "complete unions", is no more than graceful motions unless enriched by brain fucking imagination. And here is the charming enigma, the paradoxical truth that dares not show its face. Usually, even in the deepest fusions, neither partner really knows what is flashing through that delightful, adorable mind of the other.

In the future the wearing of cyberclothing will be as conventional as the wearing of body-covering clothing. To appear with out your platonic gear would be like showing up in public stark naked. A new global language of virtual-signals, icons, 3-D pixels will be the lingua franca of our species, Instead of using words, we shall communicate in self-edited movie clips selected from the chaotic jungles of images stored on our wrists.

We are talking about learning how to operate our minds, our brains, our souls.

The local vocal dialects will remain, of course, for intimate communication. Nothing from our rich, glorious past will be eliminated. When we extend our minds and empower our brains, we shall not abandon our bodies, nor our machines, nor our tender, secret love whispers.

We will drive cars, as we now ride horses, for pleasure. We will develop exquisite bodily expressions, not to work like efficient robots, but to perform acts of grace.

The main function of the human being in the 21st Century is "imagineering" and electronic-reality fabrication; to learn how to express, communicate, and share the wonders of our brains with others.

7

ARTIFICIAL INTELLIGENCE

In the Sixties, Hermann Hesse was revered by
college students and art rowdies as the voice
of the decade. He was a mega-sage, bigger than
Tolken or Salinger, McLuhan or Bucky Fuller.
Hesse's mystical, utopian novels were read by
millions. The popular, electrically amplified rock
band Steppenwolf named themselves after Hesse's
psyberdelic hero, Harry Halter, who smoked those
"long, thin yellow immeasurably enlivening and
delightful" cigarettes, then zoomed around the
Theatre of the Mind, ostensibly going where no
fictional heroes had been before.

The movie *Steppenwolf* was financed by Peter
Sprague, at that time the Egg King of Iran. I lost
the male lead to Max Van Sydow. Rosemary's
part was played by Dominique Sanda. But that
story is filed in another database.

Hesse's picaresque adventure, *The Journey
to the East,* was a biggie too. It inspired armies
of pilgrims—yours truly included—to hip-hike
somewhere East of Suez, along the Hashish
Trail to India. The goal of this Childlike Crusade? Enlightenment 101, an elective course.

Yes, it was that season for trendy Sufi mysticism, inner Hindu voyaging, breathless Buddhist searches for ultimate meaning. Poor Hesse, he seems out of place up here in the high tech, cybercool, Sharp catalogue, M.B.A., upwardly mobile 21st Century..

But our patronizing pity for the washed up Swiss sage may be premature. In the avant garde frontiers of the computer culture, around Massachusetts Avenue in Cambridge, around Palo Alto, in the Carnegie-Mellon AI labs, in the back rooms of the computer-graphics labs in Southern California, a Hesse comeback seems to be happening. This revival, however, is not connected with Hermann's mystical, eastern writings. It's based on his last, and least-understood work, Magister Ludi, or *The Glass Bead Game*.

This book, which earned Hesse the expense-paid brain ride to Stockholm, is positioned a few centuries in the future, when human intelligence is enhance and human culture elevated by a device for thought-processing called the glass-bead game.

Up here in the Electronic 2000s we can appreciate what Hesse did at the very pinnacle—Thirties and early Forties—of the smoke-stack mechanical age. He forecast with astonishing accuracy a certain postindustrial device for converting thoughts to digital elements and processing them. No doubt about it, the sage of the hippies was anticipating an electronic mind-appliance that would not appear on the consumer market until the mid-Seventies. I refer, of course, to the Fruit from the Tree of Knowledge called the Apple computer.

The Aldous Huxley-Hermann Hesse Fugue

I first heard of Hermann Hesse from Aldous Huxley. He was reading Hesse and talked a lot about his theory of human development. Huxley was Carnegie Visiting Professor at MIT. His assignment: to give a series of seven lectures on the subject, "What a Piece of Work Is Man." A couple thousand people attended each lecture. Aldous spent most of his off-duty hours hanging around the Harvard Psychedelic Drug Research project coaching us beginners in the history of mysticism and the ceremonial care and handling of LSD, which he sometimes called "gratuitous grace."

Hermann Hesse's Three Stages of Human Development.

1. The tribal sense of tropical-blissful unity,
2. The horrid polarities of the feudal industrial societies, good evil, male female, Christian-Moslem, etc., and
3. The revelatory rediscovery of The Oneness of It All.

No question about it, Hegel's three authoritarian thumbprints—thesis-antithesis-synthesis—were smudged all over the construct, but Hesse and Huxley didn't seem to worry about it, so why should we untutored Harvard psychologists?

We all dutifully set to work reading Hesse. Huxley claimed that his own spiritual intellectual development in England followed the developmental lifeline of Hesse in Germany. Aldous delighted in weaving together themes from his life that paralleled Hesse's.

Parodies of Paradise

Huxley's last book, *Island*, presents an atypical, tropical utopia in which meditation, gestalt therapy, and psychedelic ceremonies create a society of Buddhist serenity.

I spent the afternoon of November 20, 1963, at Huxley's bedside, listening carefully as the dying philosopher spoke in a soft voice about many things. He fashioned a pleasant little literary fugue as he talked about three books he called "parodies of paradise": his own *Island*, Orwell's *1984,* and Hesse's *The Glass Bead Game.*

Aldous told me with a gentle chuckle that Big Brother, the beloved dictator of Orwell's nightmare society, was based on Winston Churchill. "Remember Big Brother's spell-binding rhetoric about the blood, sweat, and fears requisitioned from everyone to defeat Eurasia? The hate sessions? Priceless satire. And the hero's name is Winston Smith,"

Aldous was, at that moment in time, fascinated by the *Tibetan Book of the Dying,* which I had just translated from Victorian English into American. The manuscript, which was later published as *The Psychedelic Experience,* was used by Laura Huxley to guide Aldous' psychedelic passing.

Huxley spoke wryly of the dismal conclusions of *Island, The Glass Bead Game*, and Orwell's classic. His own idealistic island society was crushed by industrial powers seeking oil. Hesse's utopian Castalia was doomed because it was out of touch with human realities. Then the crushing of love by the power structure in 1984. Unhappy endings. I timidly asked him if he was passing on a warning or an exhortation to me. He smiled enigmatically.

Two days later Aldous Huxley died. His passing went almost unnoticed, because John F. Kennedy also died on November 22, 1963. It was a bad day for utopians and futurists all over.

Ontological Evolution of Hermann Hesse

Hermann Hesse was born in 1877 in the little Swabian town of Caiw, Germany, the son of Protestant missionaries. His home background and education, like Huxley's, were intellectual, classical, idealistic. His life exemplified change and metamorphosis. If we accept Theodore Ziolkowski's academic perception, "Hesse's literary career parallels the development of modern literature from a fin de siècle aestheticism through expressionism to a contemporary sense of human commitment."

Voice of Romantic Escapism

Hesse's first successful novel, *Peter Camenzind*—published in 1904—reflected the frivolous sentimentality of the Gay Nineties, which, like the Roaring Twenties, offered a last fun frolic to a class society about to collapse.

"From aestheticism he shifted to melancholy realism. Hesse's novels fictionalize the admonitions of an outsider who urges us to question accepted values, to rebel against the system, to challenge conventional 'reality' in the light of higher ideals" (Ziolkowski).

Hesse made the obligatory mystical pilgrimage to India in 1911, and there, along the Ganges, picked up the microorganisms that were later to appear in a full-blown Allen Ginsbergsonian mysticism.

In 1914 Europe convulsed with nationalism and military frenzy. Hesse, like Dr. Benjamin Spock in another time warp, became an outspoken pacifist and war resister. Two months after the "outbreak of hostilities," he published an essay titled "0 Freunde, nicht dieser Tone" ["Oh Friends, Not These Tones"]. It was an appeal to the youth of Germany, deploring the stampede to disaster.

His dissenting brought him official censure and newspaper attacks. From this time on, Hesse was apparently immune to the ravages of patriotism, nationalism, and respect for authority.

Father of New-Age Psychology

Hesse's *Siddhartha* is the story of a Kerouac-Snyder manhood spent "on the road to Benares" performing feats of detached, amused, sexy one-upmanship.

In the June 1986 issue of *Playboy,* the Islamic yogic master and basketball superstar Kareen Abdul-Jabbar ("noble and powerful servant of Allah") summarized with his legendary cool the life stages he had experienced, using bead-

> **Hesse was apparently immune to the ravages of patriotism, nationalism, and respect for authority.**

game fugue techniques to weave together the
strand of his biography: basketball, racism, religion, drugs, sex, jazz, politics. "In my senior year
in high school," Abdul-Jabbar, "I started reading
everything I could get my hands on—Hindu texts,
Upanishads, Zen, Hermann Hesse—you name it!

Playboy: *"What most impressed you?"*

Abdul-Jabbar: *"Hesse's Siddhartha. I was*
then going through the same things
that Siddhartha went through in his
adolescence, and I identified with his
rebellion against established precepts
of love and life. Siddhartha becomes an
aesthetic man, a wealthy man, a sensu-
ous man—he explores all these different
worlds and doesn't find enlightenment
in any of them. That was the book's
great message to me; so I started to de-
velop my own value system as to what
was good and what wasn't."

Steppenwolf, observes Ziolkowski, was greeted
as a "psychedelic orgy of sex, drugs, and jazz."
Other observers with a more historic perspec-
tive—present company included—have seen
Steppenwolf as a final send up of the solemn
polarities of the industrial age. Hesse mocks the
Freudian conflicts, Nietzschean torments, the
Jungian polarities, the Hegelian machineries of
European civilization.

Harry Hailer enters "The Magic Theatre.
Price of Admission: Your Mind." First he engages
in a "Great Automobile Hunt," a not too subtle
rejection of the sacred symbol of the industrial
age. Behind the door marked "Guidance in the

Building-Up of the Personality. Success Guaranteed!" H. H. learns to play a post-Freudian video game in which the pixels are part of the personality. "We can demonstrate to anyone whose soul has fallen to pieces that he can rearrange these pieces of a previous self *in what order he pleases* and so attain to an endless multiplicity of moves in the game of life."

This last sentence precisely states the basis for the many postindustrial religions of self-actualization. You learn how to put together the elements of your self in what order pleases you! Then press the advance key to continue.

The mid-life crisis of the Steppenwolf, his overheated Salinger inner conflicts, his Woody Allen despairs, his unsatisfied Norman Mailer longings, are dissolved in a whirling kaleidoscope of quick flashing neurorealities. "I knew," gasps H. H., "that all the hundred pieces of life's game were in my pocket.... One day I would be a better hand at the game."

The Glass-Bead Game Converts Thoughts to Elements

What do you do after you've reduced the heavy, massive boulder-like thoughts of your mechanical culture to elements? If you're a student of physics or chemistry you rearrange the fissioned bits and pieces into new combinations. Synthetic chemistry of the mind. Hesse was hanging out in Basel, home of Paracelsus. Alchemy 101. Solve et coagule. Recompose them in new combinations. You become a master of the bead game. Let the random-number generator shuffle your thought-deck and deal out some new hands!

Understandably, Hesse never gives a detailed description of this preelectronic data-processing appliance called the bead game. But he does explain its function. Players learned how to convert decimal numbers, musical notes, words, thoughts, images into elements, glass beads that could be strung in endless abacus combinations and rhythmic-fugue sequences to create a higher level language of clarity, purity, and ultimate complexity.

Global Language Based on Digital Units

Hesse described the game as "a serial arrangement, an ordering, grouping, and interfacing of concentrated concepts from many fields of thought and aesthetics."

In time, wrote Hesse, "the Game of games had developed into a kind of universal language through which the players could express values and set these in relation to one another."

In the beginning the game was designed, constructed, and continually updated by a guild of mathematicians called Castalia. Later generations of hackers used the game for educational, intellectual, and aesthetic purposes. Eventually the game became a global science of mind, an indispensable method for clarifying thoughts and communicating them precisely.

Evolution of the Computer

Hesse, of course, was not the first to anticipate digital thought processing. Around 600 B.C. the Greek Pythagoras (music of the spheres) and the Chinese Lao (yin yang)-tzu were speculating that all reality and knowledge could and should be expressed in the play of binary numbers. In 1832 a young Englishman, George Boole, developed an algebra of symbolic logic. In the next decade Charles Babbage and Ada Countess Lovelace worked on the analytic thought-engine. A century later, exactly when Hesse was constructing his "game" in Switzerland, the brilliant English logician Alan Turing was writing about machines that could simulate thinking, AI—artificial intelligence.

Hesse's unique contribution, however, was not technical, but social. Forty-five years before Toffler and Naisbitt, Hesse predicted the emergence of an information culture. In *The Glass Bead Game* Hesse presents a sociology of computing. With the rich detail of a World-Cup novelist (he won the Nobel Prize for Literature with this book) he describes the emergence of a utopian subculture centered around the use of digital mind-appliances.

Hesse understood that a language based on mathematical elements need not be cold, impersonal, rote.

Hesse then employs his favorite appliance, parody (cyber farce), to raise the disturbing question of the class division between the computer hip and the computer illiterate. The electronic elite versus the rag-and-glue proles with their hand-operated Coronas. The dangers of a two-tier society of the information rich and the information have-nots.

Forty-five years before Toffler and Naisbitt, Hesse predicted the emergence of an information culture.

Glorification of the Castalian Hacker Culture

The Glass Bead Game is the story of Joseph Knecht, whom we meet as a brilliant grammar-school student about to be accepted into the Castalian brotherhood and educated in the intricacies of the authorized thought-processing system. The descriptions of Castalia are charmingly pedantic. The reverent reader is awed by the sublime beauty of the system and the monk-like dedication of the adepts.

The scholarly narrator explains:

> *This Game of games . . . has developed into a kind of universal speech, through the medium of which the players are able to express values in lucid symbols and to place them in relation to each other.... A game can originate, for example, from a given astronomical configuration, a theme from a Bach fugue, a phrase of Leibnitz or from the Upanishads, and the fundamental idea awakened can be built up and enriched through assonances to relative concepts. While a moderate beginner can, through these symbols, formulate parallels between a piece of classical music and the formula of a natural law, the adept and Master of the Game can lead the opening theme into the freedom of boundless combinations.*

In this last sentence, Hesse describes the theory of digital computing. The wizard programmer can convert any idea, thought, or number into binary number chains that can be sorted into all kinds of combinations. We reencounter here the age long dream of philosophers, visionary poets, and linguists of a *universitas*, a synthesis of all knowledge, the ultimate data base of ideas, a global language of mathematical precision.

Hesse understood that a language based on mathematical elements need not be cold, impersonal, rote. Reading *The Glass Bead Game* we share the enthusiasm of today's hacker-visionaries who know that painting, composing, writing, designing, innovating with clusters of electrons (beads?) offers much more creative freedom than expressions limited to print on paper, chemical paints smeared on canvas, or acoustic (i.e., mechanical-unchangeable) sounds.

Hesse's Golden Age of Mind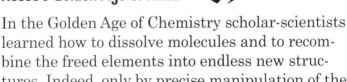

In the Golden Age of Chemistry scholar-scientists learned how to dissolve molecules and to recombine the freed elements into endless new structures. Indeed, only by precise manipulation of the play of interacting elements could chemists fabricate the marvels that have so changed our world.

In the Golden Age of Physics, physicists, both theoretical and experimental, learned how to fission atoms arid to recombine the freed particles into new elemental structures. In *The Glass Bead Game* Hesse portrays a Golden Age of Mind. The knowledge information programmers of Castalla, like chemists and physicists, dissolve thought molecules into elements (heads) and weave them into new patterns.

In his poem, *The Last Glass Bead Game,* Hesse's hero Joseph Knecht writes, "We draw upon the iconography ... that sings like crystal constellations."

Technology Invents Ideology

Hesse apparently anticipated McLuhan's First Law of Communication: The medium is the message. The technology you use to package, store, communicate your thoughts defines the limits of your thinking. Your choice of thought tool determines the limitations of your thinking. If your thought technology is words-carved-into-marble, let's face it, you're not going to be a light-hearted flexible thinker. An oil painting or a wrinkled papyrus in a Damascus library cannot communicate the meaning of a moving-picture film. New thought technology creates new ideas. The printing press created national languages, the national state, literacy, the industrial age. Television, like it or not, has produced a global thought processing very different from oral and literate cultures.

Understanding the power of technology, Hesse tells us that the new mind culture of Castalla was based on a tangible mental device, a thought machine, "a frame modeled on a child's abacus, a frame with several dozen wires on which could be strung glass beads of various sizes, shapes, and colours."

Please do not be faked out by the toy-like simplicity of this device. Hesse has changed the units of meaning, the vocabulary of thought. This is serious stuff. Once you have defined the units of thought in terms of mathematical elements you've introduced a major mutation in the intelligence of your culture.

The Evolution of the Game

 The glass-bead appliance was first used by musicians: "The wires corresponded to the lines of the musical staff, the beads to the time values of the notes."

A bare two or three decades later the game was taken over by mathematicians. For a long while indeed, a characteristic feature of the game's history was that it was constantly preferred, used, and further elaborated by whatever branch of learning happened to be experiencing a period of high development or a renaissance.

At various times the game was taken up and imitated by nearly all the scientific and scholarly disciplines. The analytic study of musical values had led to the reduction of musical events to physical and mathematical formulae. Soon afterward, philology borrowed this method and began to measure linguistic configurations as physics measures processes in nature. The visual arts soon followed suit. Each discipline that seized upon the game created its own language of formulae, abbreviations, and possible combinations.

It would lead us too far afield to attempt to describe in detail how the world of mind, after its purification, won a place for itself in the state. Supervision of the things of the mind among the people and in government came to be consigned more and more to the intellectuals. This was especially the case with the educational system.

Artificial Intelligence & Alienated Hackers

"The mathematicians brought the game to a high degree of flexibility and capacity for sublimation, so that it began to acquire something of a consciousness of itself and its possibilities".

In this last phrase, Hesse premonitors Arthur C. Clarke and Stanley Kubrick's nightmare about neurotic artificial intelligence:

> Dave: *"Open the pod doors, HAL."*
>
> HAL: *"Sorry about that, Dave. This mission is too important to be threatened by human error."*

Hesse tells us that the first generations of computer adepts created a "hacker culture," an elite sect of knowledge processors who lived within the constructions of their own minds, disdaining the outside society. Then Hesse, with uncanny insight, describes the emergence of a phenomenon that has now become the fad in the information sciences.

The Artificial-Intelligence Cult

By 1984, billions of dollars were being spent in Japan (the so-called Fifth Generation projects), in America, and in Europe to develop artificial-intelligence programs. Those nations that already suffer from a serious intelligence deficit—Soviet Eurasia and the third-world nations—seem to be left out of this significant development.

The aim of AI projects is to develop enormously complicated smart machines that can reason, deduce, and make decisions more efficiently than "human beings."

The megabuck funding comes from large bureaucracies, federal, corporate, the military, banks, insurance firms, oil companies, space agencies, medical hospital networks. The mental tasks performed by the AI machineries include:

Expert systems that provide processed information and suggest decisions based on correlating enormous amounts of data. Here the computers perform, at almost the speed of light, the work of armies of clerks and technicians.

Voice-recognition programs; the computer recognizes instructions given in spoken languages.

Robotry.

AI has become the buzzword among investors in the computer industry. There seems little doubt that reasoning programs and robots will play increasingly important roles in Western society, and, of course, Japan.

Just as the bead game became the target of outside criticism, so has there been much grumbling about the AI movement. Some have asserted that the very term "artificial intelligence" is an oxymoron; a contradiction in terms, like "military intelligence."

Other critics point out that Al programs have little to do with individual human beings. These megamillion-dollar machines cannot be applied to solve personal problems, to help Ashley get a date on Friday night, to help Dieadra's problem with self-esteem. AI systems are designed to think like super-committees of experts. Remember the decision that it was cheaper to pay off a few large injury/death claims than to change the position of the gas tank on the Ford? Recall those Pentagon figures about "tolerable loss of civilian lives in a nuclear war"? That's why many feel that these toys of top management are more artificial than intelligent.

As it turns out, our HAL paranoias are exaggerated.

Computers will not replace real people. They will replace middle-and low-level bureaucrats. They will replace you only to the extent that you use artificial—rather than natural—intelligence in your life and work. If you think like a bureaucrat, a functionary, a manager, an unquestioning member of a large organization, or a chess player, beware: You may soon be out-thought!

Natural Intelligence

Humanists in the computer culture claim that there is only one form of intelligence natural intelligence, brain power which resides in the skulls of individual human beings. This wetware is genetically wired and experientially programmed to manage the personal affairs of one person, the owner, and to exchange thoughts with others.

All thought-processing tools, hand operated pencils, printed books, electronic computers can be used as extensions of natural intelligence. They are appliances for packaging, storing, communicating ideas: mirrors that reflect back what the user has thought. As Douglas Hofstadter put it in *Gödel Escher Bach*: "The self comes into being at the moment it has the power to reflect itself." And that power, Hesse and McLuhan, is determined by the thought tool used by the culture.

Individual human beings can be controlled, managed by thinking machines—computers or bead games—only to the extent that they voluntarily choose to censor their own independent thinking.

Magister Ludi Questions Authority

In the last chapters of *The Glass Bead Game* the hero, Joseph Knecht, has risen to the highest post in the Castalian order. He is "Magister Ludi, Master of the Glass Bead Game".

The game, by this time, has become a global artificial-intelligence system that runs the educational system, the military, science, engineering, mathematics, physics, linguistics, and above all, aesthetics. The great cultural ceremonies are public thought games watched with fascination by the populace.

At this moment of triumph the Mind Master begins to have doubts. He worries abut the two-tier-society in which the Castalian "computer" elite run the mind games of society, far removed from the realities of human life. The Castalians, we recall, have dedicated themselves totally to the life of the mind, renouncing power, money, family, individuality. A Castalian is the perfect "organization man", a monk of the new religion of artificial intelligence. Knecht is also concerned about the obedience, the loss of individual choice.

Hesse seems to be sending warning signals that are relevant to the situation in 1986. First, he suggests that human beings tend to center their religions on the thought-processing device their culture uses. The word of God has to come though normal channels or it won't be understood, from the stone tablet of Moses to the mass produced industrial product that is the "Good Book" of fundamentalist Christians and Moslems.

Second, control of the thought-processing machinery means control of society. The underlying antiestablishment tone of *The Glass Bead Game* must surely have caught the attention of George Orwell, another prophet of the information society. Like Joseph Knecht, Winston Smith, the hero of *1984*, works in the Ministry of Truth, reprogramming the master data base of history. Smith is enslaved by the information tyranny from which Hesse's hero tries to escape.

Third, Hesse suggests that the emergence of new intelligence machines will create new religions. The Castalian order is reminiscent of the mediaeval monastic cults, communities of hackers with security clearances, who knew the machine language, Latin, and who created and guarded the big mainframe illuminated manuscripts located in the palaces of bishops and dukes.

Most important, Hesse indicated the appropriate response of the individual who cannot accept the obedience and sell—renunciation demanded by the artificial—intelligence priesthood.

To Act As My Heart and Reason Command

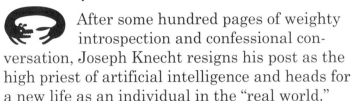 After some hundred pages of weighty introspection and confessional conversation, Joseph Knecht resigns his post as the high priest of artificial intelligence and heads for a new life as an individual in the "real world."

He explains his "awakening" in a letter to the Order. After thirty years of major league thought processing, Knecht has come to the conclusion that organizations maintain themselves by rewarding obedience with privilege! With the blinding force of a mystical experience Knecht suddenly sees that the Castalian AI community "had been infected by the characteristic disease of elite-hood-hubris, conceit, class arrogance, sell righteousness, exploitiveness. . ."!

And, irony of all irony, the member of such a thought-processing bureaucracy "often suffers from a severe lack of insight into his place in the structure of the nation, his place in the world and world history." Before we rush to smile at such platitudes about bureaucratic myopia and greed, we should remember that Hesse wrote this book during the decade when Hitler, Stalin, and Mussolini were terrorizing Europe with totalitarianism. The cliché Athenian-democratic maxim "think for yourself; question authority"

was decidedly out of fashion, even in civilized
countries like Switzerland.

Gentle consideration for the touchiness of the
times was, we assume, the reason why Hesse,
the master of parody, leads his timid readers with such a slow, formal tempo to the final
confrontation between Alexander, the president
of the Order, and the dissident game master. In
his most courteous manner Knecht explains to
Alexander that he will not accept obediently the
"decision from above."

The president gasps in disbelief. And we can
imagine most of the thought-processing elite of
Europe, the professors, the intellectuals, the linguists, the literary critics, and news editors join-
ing Alexander when he sputters, "not prepared
to accept obediently ... an unalterable decision
from above? Have I heard you right, Magister?"

Later, Alexander asks in a low voice, "And
how do you act now?"

"As my heart and reason command," replies
Joseph Knecht.

The best way to understand the evolution of the human race is in terms of how well we have learned to operate our brain.

8

OPERATE YOUR BRAIN

The human brain—the most infinitely and imaginatively complex knowledge system— has a hundred billion neurons, and each neuron has the knowledge-processing capacity of a powerful computer. The human brain has more connections than there are atoms in the universe. It has taken us thousands of years to even realize that we don't understand the chaotics of this complexity. The human brain can process more than a hundred million signals a second and counting.

The best way to understand the evolution of the human race is in terms of how well we have learned to operate our brain. If you think about it, we're basically brains. Our bodies are here to move our brains around. Our bodies are equipped with all these sensory inputs and output ports to bring information into the neurocomputer. In just the last decade, our species has multiplied the ability to use our brains by a thousand fold.

The way to understand how efficiently you're using your brain is to clock it in rpm—*realities per minute.* Just on the basis of input/output, my brain is now operating at a hundred times more rpm than in 1960.

When we were back in the caves a million or so years ago, we were just learning to chip stones to make tools. We lived on a planet where everything was natural. There was almost nothing artificial or even handmade—but we had the same brains. Each of our ancient ancestors carried around an enormously complex brain that eventually fissioned the atom, sent human beings to the Moon, and created rock video. Long ago we had the same brains, but we weren't using the abilities. If the brain is like a computer, then the trick is to know how to format your brain—to set up operating systems to run your brain.

If you are a computer, you have a choice. You can have word processing or not. If you have word processing, you have choices of which program to run. Once you've formatted your brain, trained your brain with that method, you have to go through that program to use it. The process of formatting your brain is called *imprinting.*

The process of formatting your brain is called imprinting.

Imprinting

Imprinting is a multimedia input of data. For a baby, it's the warmth of the mother, the softness, the sound, the taste of the breast. That's called booting up or formatting. Now baby's brain is hooked to Mama and then of course from Mama to Daddy, food, etc., but it's the Mama file that's the first imprint.

There is the ability to boot up or add new directions. To activate the brain is called *yogic* or *psychedelic*. To transmit what's in the brain is cybernetic. The brain, we are told by neurologist, has between seventy and a hundred buttons known as receptor sites that can imprint different circuits. Certain biochemical—usually botanical—products activate those particular parts of the brain.

In tribal times, before written language, communication was effected through the human voice, small groups, and body motion. Most pagan tribes had rituals that occurred at harvest time, in the springtime, or at the full Moon. The tribe came together and activated a collective boot-up system. They hooked all their computers to the same tribal language. This often involved the use of psychedelic plants.

When you think of it, the ultimate wicked oxymoron is organized religion. Imagine a group of control-freak men getting together and saying: 'We're going to impose our order on the fifteen-billion-year evolutionary chaotic process that's happening on this planet, and all over the galaxy. We're going to chisel out the rules of a bureaucracy to keep us in power."

In terms of modern computers and electronic devices, this would be a multimedia imprinting ceremony. The fire was the center of light and heat. There were symbolic objects, such as feathers or bones. This experience booted up

A human being is basically a tribal person, the brains of all present so they could share the basic tribal system. But each person could have his own vision quest. He could howl like a wolf, hoot like an owl, roll around like a snake. Each tribal member was learning how to activate, operate, boot up, and accept the uniqueness of his/her own brain.

A human being is basically a tribal person, most comfortable being together in small groups facilitating acceptance and understanding of each other as individuals. Later forms of civilization have discredited individualism. The history of the evolution of the human spirit has to do with new methods of media, communication, or language.

Communication Control

About five thousand years ago, after the species got pretty good with tools and building, somewhere in the Middle East—possibly also in China—people began making marks on shells and on pieces of papyrus. This allowed for long-distance communication. Handwriting, which linked up hundreds of thousands of people, gave total power to the people who knew how to control the writing. Marshall McLuhan reminded us that throughout human history, whoever controls the media controls the people. This is French semiotics. Literacy is used to control the poor. The educated use literacy to control the uneducated.

A typical feudal organization, such as the Catholic Church, restricted the power to send a message like this to a very special class of computer hacker-nerds called monks. Only they were authorized to touch the mainframe—the illuminated manuscripts up in the castle of the duke or cardinal. But to the others—no matter how important a person in the village or the city—the word came down from the Higher Ups.

Once people start organizing in large groups of thousands, or hundreds of thousands, the tribal situation could no longer be controlled. If a hundred thousand people are all hooked up, like a hive or termite colony, there has to be some central organization that keeps it going.

With thousands of people carrying rocks to build a pyramid, or thousands of people building the churches of the pope, a feudal society can't function if the workers are accessing their singular brain programs. To illustrate the totalitarian power control of the feudal situation, consider the basic metaphor of the "shepherd" and the "sheep." "The Lord is my shepherd; I shall not want. He maketh me to he down in green pastures." Now, if the Lord is your shepherd, who the fuck are you? Bah! Even today, when the pope flies around to third-world countries, they speak of "the pope and his flock."

Bible as Brain Control

Another example of brain control preventing the individual from accessing his or her own computer is the first chapter of the *Bible.* The opening text of Genesis lays it right out. God says,

"I made the skies. I made the planets, I made
the earth, I made the water, I made the land. I
made the creepy-crawly things, and I made you,
Adam, to be in my likeness, and I put you in the
ultimate destination resort, which is the Garden
of Eden. Boy, you can do anything you want. I'm
going to pull out a rib and give you a helpmate
like a little kitchen slave, named Eve. You can
do whatever you want, Adam. This is paradise.

"However, there are two Food and Drug regula-
tions. See that tree over there? That's the Tree of
Immortality. It offers cryonics and cloning. You shall
not eat of the fruit of that lest you become a God like
me and live forever. You see that tree over there.
That's even more dangerous. You shall not eat of the
fruit of that because that is the Tree of Knowledge. It
offers expansions of consciousness."

Genesis makes it clear that the whole universe is owned, operated, controlled, and fabricated by one God—and he's a big, bad-tempered
male. That's why we have a war on mind drugs.
The one thing that no mass society can stand is
individuals and small groups that go off to start
learning how to program, reprogram, boot up,
activate, and format their own brains.

There's a good reason for these taboos. The feudal and industrial stages of evolution are similar
to the stages in the evolution of individuals. Young
children are glad to have Daddy be shepherd, but
after a while the child has to take responsibility.

Feudal societies imprinted millions to totally
devote their lives to being herd flock animals,
imagine living on a farm fifty miles from Chartres
during the 15th Century. On Sundays you walked

five miles to get to a little village. There the priest told you, "Listen, six months from now we're all going to Chartres. There's going to be a big ceremony because the archbishop will be there."

The one thing that no mass society can stand is individuals and small groups that go off to start learning how to program, reprogram, boot up, activate, and format their own brains.

You spent a week to hike there. You walked into the central square of Chartres. You looked up and saw a cathedral taller than any trees, almost like a mountain, with its stained-glass windows and statues, and there were all those people the priest told you about. They're seven or ten feet tall. You walked in, looked up at the towering Gothic arches, the rose windows, heard the organ music and chanting, smelled the incense.

Talk about multi-sensory, multimedia imprinting! If you thought that the Grateful Dead light show was something, for almost two thousand years the wizards of the Catholic Church orchestrated one hell of a show. The smell of perfume, the candles, the chanting getting louder and louder, until suddenly the bishop appeared, bejeweled, carried in on a big golden throne. You'd never seen anything like that back on the farm.

An earlier multimedia imprinting event took place near Athens before the birth of Christ. The Eleusinian mystery rite was an annual religious event that reoccurred for over a thousand years. The wisest people as well as ordinary folk came

You create the realities you inhabit. to the temple of Eleusis to participate in the secret ceremony. An LSD-type drink made from ergot of barley was drunk by all the initiates. An extravagant light show and a powerful dramatic reenactment was performed, resulting in a group experience of chaos and rebirth for the audience.

It's no accident that the Greek philosophers, dramatists, and poets left an incredible record of creative self-expression and polytheism. When Socrates said, "The function of human life is to know yourself; intelligence is virtue," he was invoking the Greek notion of humanism that was to later influence the Renaissance and the romantic periods.

Far more than by weapons, society is controlled by multimedia, neurological imprinting. Marshall McLuhan reminded us that the medium is the message.

When Gutenberg invented moveable type, it empowered dukes and cardinals to print and distribute thousands of Bibles and histories of the Crown. Within a few decades, many Europeans were learning how to do what only the monks could do. Gutenberg created the one device that was basic to the future industrial—factory civilization—mass production for consumers.

In the industrial age, the virtuous person was good, prompt, reliable, dependable, efficient, directed, and, of course, replaceable. There was not much need for the individual to operate his or her own brain in a factory civilization. The bosses can't have people on an assembly line becoming too creative, as in the Cheech and Chong movie where cars are coming down the line.

Cheech & Chong Workin'

Hey, Cheech, I'm gonna go eat now."
"You can't, not yet." "Why not?"
"You can't eat until the bell rings."
"Okay, let's paint the next car rainbow."

You cannot operate industrial society with too much individuality and access to the multimedia capacities of the brain.

Around 1900 Einstein came up with the idea that space and time only exist in an interactive field, and Max Planck devised a theory that the basic elements of the universe are particles of information. Then came Heisenberg's proof that you create your own reality. And a new philosophy emerged called *quantum physics*, which suggests that the individual's function is to inform and be informed. You really exist only when you're in a field sharing and exchanging information. You create the realities you inhabit.

What's the brain for? Why do we have this incredible instrument? Our brains want to be hooked up with other brains. My brain is only in operation when she's slamming back and forth bytes and bits of information. Multimedia intercommunication.

The original basic dream of humanity is that the individual has divinity within. There is this enormous power within our bio-computer brains. We are going to have to learn how to use this power, how to boot it up.

9

BOOT UP YOUR BIO-COMPUTER

The human brain, we are told, is a galaxy of over a hundred billion neurons, any two of which can organize and communicate as much complex information as a mainframe computer.

Many cognitive psychologists now see the brain as a universe of information processors. Our minds, according to this metaphor, serve as the software that programs the neural hardware—or wetware. Most of the classic psychological terms can now be redefined in terms of computer concepts. Cognitive functions like memory, forgetting, learning, creativity, and logical thinking are now studied as methods by which the mind forms "data bases" and stores, processes, shuffles, and retrieves information.

Noncognitive functions such as emotions, moods, sensory perceptions, hallucinations, obsessions, phobias, altered states, possession trance experiences, glossolalias, intoxications, visionary images, and psychedelic perspectives can now be viewed in terms of ROM brain circuits or autonomous-sympathetic-midbrain sectors that are usually not accessed by left-brain or forebrain conscious decision. These nonlinear, unconscious areas can, as we well know, be activated intentionally or involuntarily by various means. The pop term "turn on" carries the fascinating cybernetic implication that one can selectively dial up or access brain sectors that process specific channels of information signals normally unavailable.

These concepts could emerge only in an electronic culture. The mystics and altered-state philosophers of the past, like the Buddha or St. John of the Cross or William James or Aldous Huxley, could not describe their visions and illuminations and ecstasies and enlightenments in terms of "turning on" electronic appliances.

Computers Help Understand the Brain

There is no naïve assumption here that the brain is a computer. However, by using cybernetic terminology to describe mind and brain functions, we can add to our knowledge about the varieties of thought-processing experiences.

This use of a manufactured artifact like the computer to help us understand internal biological processes seems to be a normal stage in the growth of human knowledge. Harvey's notions about the heart as pump and the circulation of the blood obviously stemmed from hydraulic engineering. Our understanding of metabolism and nutrition inside the body had to await the science of thermodynamics and energy machines.

Two hundred years ago, before electrical appliances were commonplace, the brain was vaguely defined as an organ that secreted "thoughts" the way the heart processed blood and the lungs processed air. In the 1950s my Psychology 101 professors described the brain in terms of the most advanced information system available—an enormous telephone exchange. This metaphor obviously did not lead to profitable experimentation; so the brain was generally ignored by psychology. The psychoanalytic theories of Freud were more useful and comprehensible, because they were based on familiar thermodynamic principles: Neurosis was caused by the blocking or repression of surging, steamy, over-heated dynamic instincts that exploded or leaked out in various symptomatic behavior.

During the early Sixties our Harvard Psychedelic Drug Research project studied the reactions of thousands of subjects during psilocybin and LSD sessions. We were able to recognize and classify the standard range of psychedelic-hallucinogenic experiences, and to distinguish them from the effects of other drugs like uppers, downers, booze, opiates, tranquilizers. But we were able to categorize them only in terms of subjective reactions. There was simply no scientific language to communicate or model for the wide range and "strange" effects of these chaotic phenomena. Psychiatrists, policemen, moralists, and people who did not use drugs accepted the notion of "psychotomimetic states." There was one normal way to see the world. Chaotic drugs caused all users to lose their grasp on the one-and-only authorized reality, thus mimicking insanity.

Looking to Mysticism

To talk and think about drug-induced experiences, the Harvard drug experimenters and other researchers were forced to fall back on the ancient literature of Christian mysticism and those oriental yogic disciplines that had studied visionary experiences for centuries. The scholars of mysticism and spiritual transcendence snobbishly tended to view "normal reality" as a web of socially induced illusions. They tended to define, as the philosophic religious goal of life, the attainment of altered states.

Needless to say, enormous confusion was thus created. Most sensible, practical Americans were puzzled and irritated by this mad attempt on the part of the mystical millions to enthusiastically embrace chemical insanity and self-induced chaotics. Epistemological debates about the definition of reality soon degenerated into hysterical social extremism on the part of almost all concerned, present company included. Arguments about the nature of reality are always heavy, often bitter and emotional. Cultural, moral, political, racial, and above all, generational issues were involved in the Drug Wars of the late 20th Century.

But the basic problem was semiotic. Debate collapsed into emotional babble because there was no language or conceptual model of what happened when you got "high", "stoned", "fucked up", loaded", "wasted", "blessed", "spaced out", "illuminated", "satirized," "god-intoxicated", etc.

Those young, bright baby-boom Americans, who had been dialing and tuning television screens since infancy, and who had learned how to activate and turn on their brains using chaotic drugs in serious introspective experiments, were uniquely prepared to engineer the interface between the computer and the cybernetic organ known as the human brain.

Here again, external technology can provide us with an updated model and language to understand inner neuro-function. Television became popularized in the 1950s. Many psychedelic trippers of the next decades tended to react like television viewers passively watching the pictures flashing on their mind-screens. The semantic level of the acid experimenters was defined by the word "Wow!" The research groups I worked with at Harvard, Millbrook, and Berkeley fell back on gaseous, oriental, Genges-enlightenment terminology for which I humbly apologize.

Then, in the Seventies, the Apple computer was introduced. At the same time video games, provided young people with a hands-on experience of moving flashy electronic, digital information around on screens. It was no accident that many of the early designers and marketers of these electronic appliances lived in the San Francisco area and tended to be intelligent adepts in the use of psychedelic drugs.

Those young, bright baby-boom Americans, who had been dialing and tuning television screens since infancy, and who had learned how to activate and turn on their brains using chaotic drugs in serious introspective experiments, were uniquely prepared to engineer the interface between the computer and the cybernetic organ known as the human brain. They could handle accelerated thought-processing, multilevel realities, instantaneous chains of digital logic much more comfortably than their less-playful, buttoned-up, conservative, MBA rivals at IBM. Much of Steve Jobs's astonishing success in developing the Apple and the MAC was explicitly motivated by his crusade against IBM, seen as the archenemy of the 1960s culture.

In the Eighties, millions of young Americans became facile in digital thought-processing using inexpensive home computers. Most of them intuitively understood that the best model for understanding and operating the mind came from the mix of psychedelic and cybernetic cultures.

Hundreds of New-Age pop psychologists, like Werner Erhard and Shirley MacLane, taught folks how to re-program their minds, write the scripts of their lives, upgrade thought-processing. At the same time the new theories of imprinting, i.e., sudden programming of the brain, were popularized by ethologists and hip psychologists like Conrad Lorenz, Niko Tinbergen, and John Lilly.

Once again, external engineered tools helped us understand inner function. If the brain is viewed as bio-hardware, and psychedelic drugs become "neurotransmitters," and if you can reprogram your mind, for better or for worse, by "turning on", then

It was no accident that many of the early designers and marketers of these electronic appliances lived in the San Francisco area and tended to be intelligent adepts in the use of psychedelic drugs, new concepts and techniques of instantaneous psychological change become possible.

Another relevant question arises. Can the computer screen create altered states? Is there a digitally induced 'high'? Can psychedelic electrons be packaged like chemicals to strike terror into the heart of the White House? Do we need a Digital Enforcement Agency (DEA) to teach kids to say "No", or more politely, "No, thank you" to RAM pushers?

My opinion is in the negative. But what do I know? I am currently enjoying a mild digital dependence, but it seems manageable and socially useful. I follow the ancient Sufi-Pythagorean maxim regarding creative writing:

> *"If thou write stoned, edit straight. If thou write straight, edit stoned."*

........and always with a team.

10

CYBERFREEDOM

O nce upon a time . . . knowledge-information was stored in extremely expensive mainframe systems called illuminated volumes, usually Bibles, carefully guarded in the palace of the duke or bishop, and accessible only to security-cleared, socially-alienated hackers called monks. Then in 1456 Johannes Gutenberg invented a most important piece of hardware: the moveable-type printing press. This knowledge-information processing system could mass-produce inexpensive, portable software readily available for home use: The Personal Book.

Until recently, computers were in much the same sociopolitical situation as the pre-Gutenberg systems.The mainframe knowledge-processors that ran society were the monopoly of governments and large corporations. They were carefully guarded by priestly technicians with security clearances. The average person, suddenly thrust into electronic illiteracy and digital helplessness, was understandably threatened.

The Mainframe Monopoly

My first contact with computers came in 1950, when I was director of a Kaiser Foundation psychological research project that developed mathematical profiles for the interpersonal assessment of personality. In line with the principles of humanistic psychology the aim of this research was to free persons from dependency on doctors, professionals, institutions, and diagnostic-thematic interpretations. To this end, we elicited clusters of yes-no responses form subjects and fed back knowledge in the from of profiles and indices to the patients themselves.

Relying on dimensional information rather than interpretative categories, our research was ideally suited to computer analysis. Routinely we sent stacks of data to the Kaiser Foundation's computer room, where mysterious technicians converted our numbers into relevant indices. Computers were thus helpful, but distant and unapproachable. I distrusted the mainframes because I saw them as devices that would merely increase the dependence of individuals upon experts.

In 1960 I became a director of the Harvard Psychedelic Drug Research program. The aims of this project were also humanistic: to teach individuals how to self-administer psychoactive drugs in order to free their psyches without reliance upon doctors or institutions. Again we used mainframes to index responses to questionnaires about drug experiences, but I saw no way for this awesome knowledge-power to be put in the hands of individuals. I know now that our research with psychedelic drugs and, in fact, the drug culture itself was a forecast of, or preparation for, the personal-computer age. Indeed, it was a brilliant LSD researcher, John Lilly, who in 1972 wrote the seminal monograph on the brain as a knowledge-information processing system: *Programming and Metaprogramming in the Human Biocomputer.* Psychedelic drugs expose one to the raw experience of chaotic brain function, with the protections of the mind temporarily suspended. We are talking here about the tremendous acceleration of images, the crumbling of analogic perceptions into vapor trails of neuron off-on flashes, the multiplication of disorderly mind programs slipping in and out of awareness like floppy disks.

The seven million Americans who experienced the awesome potentialities of the brain via LSD certainly paved the way for the computer society. It is no accident that the term "LSD" was used twice in *Time* magazine's cover story about Steve Jobs, for it was Jobs and his fellow Gutenberger, Stephen Wozniak, who hooked up the personal brain with the personal computer and thus made a new culture possible.

Hands On/Tune In

The development of the personal computer was a step of Gutenberg magnitude. Just as The Personal Book transformed formed human society from the muscular-feudal to the mechanical-industrial, so has the personal electronic-knowledge processor equipped the individual to survive and evolve into the age of information. To guide us in this confusing and scary transition, it is most useful to look back and see what happened during the Gutenberg mutation. Religion was the unifying force that held feudal society together. It was natural, therefore, that the first Personal Books would be Bibles. When the religion market was satiated, many entrepreneurs wondered what other conceivable use could be made of this newfangled software.

How-to-read books were the next phase. Then came game books. It is amusing to note that the second book printed in the English language was on chess—a game that became, with its knights and bishops and kings and queens, the Pac Man of late feudalism. We can see this same pattern repeating during the current transition. Since money/business is the unifying force of the industrial age, the first Wozniak bibles were, naturally enough, accounting spreadsheets. Then came word processors, and games.

The history of human evolution is the record of technological innovation. Expensive machinery requiring large group efforts for operation generally becomes a tool of social repression by the state. The tower clock. The galley ship. The cannon. The tank. Instruments that can be owned and operated by individuals inevitably produce democratic revolutions. The bronze dagger. The crossbow. The pocket watch. The automobile as self-mover. This is the liberating "hands-on" concept. "Power to the people" means personal technology available to the individual. D.I.Y.— Do It Yourselves.

Evolution/Revolution

Digital-graphic appliances are developing a partnership between human brains and computers. In evolving to more physiological complexity, our bodies formed symbioses with armies of digestive bacteria necessary for survival. In similar fashion, our brains are forming neural-electronic symbiotic linkups with solid-state computers.

It is useful to distinguish here between addictions and symbiotic partnerships. The body can become passively addicted to certain molecules, e.g., of heroin, and the brain can become passively addicted to electronic signals, e.g., from television. The human body, as we have noted, also requires symbiotic partnerships with certain unicellular organisms.

At this point in human evolution, more and more people are developing mutually dependent, interactive relationships with their microsystems. When this happens, there comes a moment when the individual is "hooked" and cannot imagine living without the continual interchange of electronic signals between the personal brain and the personal computer.

There are interesting political implications. In the near future, more than twenty million Americans will use computers to establish intense interactive

If we are to stay free, we must see to it that the right to own digital data processors becomes as inalienable as the constitutional guarantees of free speech and a free press.

partnerships with other inhabitants of cyberspace. These individuals will operate at a level
of intelligence that is qualitatively different from
those who use static forms of knowledge-information processing. In America, this difference is
already producing a generation gap, i.e., a species
gap. After Gutenberg, Personal Books created a
new level of individual thinking that revolution-
ized society. An even more dramatic mutation in
human intelligence will occur as the new digital
light appliances permit individuals to communicate with individuals in other lands

Childhood's End?

It seems clear that we are facing one of
those genetic crossroads that have occurred so frequently in the history of primates.
The members of the human gene pool who form
symbiotic links with solid state computers will
be characterized by extremely high individual
intelligence and will settle in geographic niches
that encourage individual access to knowledge-
information-processing software.

New associations of individuals linked by
computers will surely emerge. Information nets
will encourage a swift, free interchange among
individuals. Feedback peripherals will dramatically expand the mode of exchange from keyboard
punching to neurophysiological interaction.

The keyword is, of course, "interaction." The
intoxicating power of interactive software is
that it eliminates dependence on the enormous
bureaucracy of knowledge professionals that
flourished in the industrial age. In the factory

culture, guilds and unions and associations of knowledge-workers jealously monopolized the flow of information. Educators, teachers, professors, consultants, psychotherapists, librarians, managers, journalists, editors, writers, labor unions, medical groups all such roles are now threatened.

It is not an exaggeration to speculate about the development of very different postindustrial societies. Solid-state literacy will be almost universal in America and the other Western democracies. The rest of the world, especially the totalitarian countries, will be kept electronically illiterate by their rulers. At least half the United Nations' members now prohibit or limit personal possession. And, as the implications of personal computers become more clearly understood, restrictive laws will become more apparent. If we are to stay free, we must see to it that the right to own digital data processors becomes as inalienable as the constitutional guarantees of free speech and a free press.

> **If we are to stay free, we must see to it that the right to own digital data processors becomes as inalienable as the constitutional guarantees of free speech and a free press.**

Psychedelic drugs expose one to the raw experience of chaotic brain function, with the protections of the mind temporarily suspended. We are talking here about the tremendous acceleration of images, the crumbling of analogic perceptions into vapor trails of neuron off-on flashes, the multiplication of disorderly mind programs slipping in and out of awareness like floppy disks.

11

QUANTUM JUMPS

The great philosophic achievement of the 20th Century was the discovery, made by nuclear and quantum physicists around 1900, that the visible tangible reality is written in BASIC. We seem to inhabit a universe made up of a small number of elements particles bits that swirl in chaotic clouds, occasionally clustering together in geometrically logical temporary configurations.

The solid Newtonian universe involving such immutable concepts as mass, force, momentum, and inertia, all bound into a Manichaean drama involving equal reactions of good versus evil, gravity versus levity, and entropy versus evolution, produced such pious Bank of England notions as conservation of energy. This General Motors's universe, which was dependable, dull, and predictable, became transformed in the hands of Einstein/Planck into digitized, shimmering quantum screens of electronic probabilities.

Chalk: A soft, white, grey, or buff limestone composed chiefly of the shells of foraminifers.

Quantum: The quantity or amount of something; an indivisible unit of energy; the particle mediating a specific type of elemental interaction.

Quantum Jump: Any abrupt change or step, especially in knowledge or information.

Chaos: The basic state of the universe and the human brain.

Personal Computer: A philosophic digital appliance that allows the individual to operate and communicate in the quantum information age.

By the end of the 20th century we were navigating in a reality of which Niels Bohr and Werner Heisenberg could only dream, and which Marshall McLuhan predicted. It turns out that the universe described in their psychedelic equations is best understood as a super mainframe constellation of information processor with subprograms and temporary ROM states, macros called galaxies, stars; minis called planets; micros called organisms; metamicros known as molecules, atoms, particles; and, last, but not least, micros called Macintosh.

It seems to follow that the great technological challenge of the 20th Century was to produce an inexpensive appliance that would make the chaotic universe "user friendly," which would allow the individual human to digitize, store, process, and reflect the subprograms that make up his/her own personal realities

Murmur the name "Einstein," put your hand reverently on your mouse, and give it an admiring pat. Your modest, faithful, devoted Mac is an evolutionary celebrity! It may be an advance as important as the opposable thumb, face to face lovemaking, the Model T Ford, the printing press! Owning it defines you as member of a new breed—postindustrial, postbiological, post-human—because your humble VM (Volks-Mac) permits you to think and act in terms of clusters of electrons. It allows you to cruise around in the chaotic post-Newtonian information ocean, to think and communicate in the lingua franca of the universe, the binary dialect of galaxies and atoms. Light.

A Philosophic Appliance

The chain of events that elevated us to this new genetic status, Homo sapiens electronicus, began around the turn of the century.

Physicists are traditionally assigned the task of sorting out the nature of reality. So it was Einstein, Planck, Heisenberg, Bohr, et al., who figured out that the units of energy/matter were subatomic particles that zoom around in clouds of ever changing, off-on, 0-1, yin-yang probabilities.

Einstein and the quantum physicists digitized our universe, reduced our solid realities into clusters of pixels, into recursive stairways of Godel-Escher-Bach paradox. No one understood, at first, what they were talking about. They

Quantum physics is quite literally a wild acid. trip!

expressed their unsettling theories in complex equations written on blackboards with chalk. These great physicists thought and communicated with a neolithic tool: chalk marks on the blackboard of the cave. The paradox was this: Einstein and his brilliant colleagues could not experience or operate or communicate at a quantum electronic level. In a sense they were idiot savants, able to produce equations about chaos and relativity without being able to maintain interpersonal cyberrelationships with others.

Imagine if Max Planck, paddling around in his chalkboard skin-canoe, had access to a video arcade game! He'd see right away that the blips on Centipede and the zaps of Space invaders could represent the movement of the particles that he tried to describe in chalk-dust symbols on his blackboard.

Reflect on the head-aching adjustment required here. The universe described by Einstein and the nuclear physicists is alien and terrifying. Chaotic. Quantum physics is quite literally a wild acid trip! It postulates a hallucinatory Alice-in-Wonderland universe in which everything is changing. As Heisenberg and Jimi Hendrix said, "Nothing is certain except uncertainty." Matter is energy. Energy is matter at various forms of acceleration. Particles dissolve into waves. There is no up or down in a four-dimensional movie. It all depends on your attitude, i.e., your angle of approach to the real worlds of chaotics.

In 1910, the appliance we call the universe was not user friendly and there was no hands-on manual of operations. No wonder people felt helpless and superstitious. People living in the solid, mechanical world of 1910 could no more understand or experience an Einsteinian universe than Queen Victoria could levitate or fish could read and write English. Einstein was denounced as evil and immoral by Catholic bishops and sober theologians who sensed how unsettling and revolutionary these new ideas could be.

In retrospect we see that the first seventy five years of the 20th Century were devoted to preparing, training, and initiating human beings to communicate in quantum speak, i.e., to think and act at an entirely different level in terms of digital clusters.

The task of preparing human culture for new realities has traditionally been performed by tribal communicators called artists, entertainers, performers. When Greek philosophers came up with notions of humanism, individuality, and liberty, it was the painters and sculptors of Athens who produced the commercial logos, the naked statues of curvy Venus and sleek Mercury and the other randy Olympian Gods.

When the feudal, anti-human monotheisms—Christian-Islamic—took over, it was the "nerdy" monks and

> The task of preparing human culture for new realities has traditionally been performed by tribal communicators called artists, entertainers, performers.

painters who produced the commercial artwork of the Middle Ages. God as a bearded king swathed in robes. Madonna and Bleeding Saints and crucified Jesus, wall-to-wall anguished martyrs. These advertising logos were necessary, of course, to convince the serfs to submit to the All Powerful Lord. You certainly can't run a kingdom or empire with bishops, popes, cardinals, abbots, and chancellors of the exchequer joyously running around bare-assed like Athenian pantheists.

The Renaissance was a humanist revival preparing Europeans for the industrial age. When Gutenberg invented the cheap, portable, rag-and-glue home computer known as the printing press, individuals had to be encouraged to read and write and "do it yourself!" Off came the clothes! Michelangelo erected a statue of David, naked as a jay bird, in the main square of Florence. Why David? He was the young, punk kid who stood up against Goliath, the Wed Rambo hit man of the Philistine empire.

With this historical perspective we can see that the 20th Century produced an avalanche of artistic, literary, musical, and entertainment movements, all of which shared the same goal: to strip off the robes and uniforms; to dissolve our blind faith in static structure; to loosen up the rigidities of the industrial culture; to prepare us to deal with paradox, with altered states of perception, with multidimensional definitions of nature; to make quantum reality comfortable, manageable, homey, livable; to get you to feel at home while bouncing electrons around your computer screen. Radio. Telegraph. Television. Computers.

Digital Art: Do It Yourself!

In modern art we saw the emergence of schools that dissolved reality represen- tation into a variety of subjective, relativistic attitudes. Impressionists used random spots of color and brush strokes, converting matter to reflected light waves. Seurat and the Pointillists actually painted in pixels.

Expressionism offered a quantum reality that was almost totally spontaneous. Do It Yourself! (D.I.Y.) Cubism sought to portray common ob- jects in planes and volumes reflecting the under- lying geometric structure of matter, thus directly illustrating the new physics. The Dada and col- lage movements broke up material reality into diverse bits and bytes.

Surrealism produced a slick, smooth-plastic fake reality that was later perfected by Sony. In Tokyo I have listened to electronic anthropolo- gists argue that Dali's graphic "The Persistence of Memory"—featuring melting watches—cre- ated modern Japanese culture, which no one can deny is eminently surreal.

These avant garde aesthetic D.I.Y. experi- ments were quickly incorporated into pop art, advertising, and industrial design. Society was learning to live with the shifting-screen perspec- tives and pixillated representations of the uni- verse that had been predicted by the equations of the quantum physicists. When the Coca-Cola company uses the digitized face of Max Head- room as its current logo, then America is com- fortably living in a quantum universe.

Hacking Away at the Word Line

These same aesthetic trends appeared in English literature. Next time you boot up your Mac, breathe a word of gratitude to Emerson, Stein, Yeats, Pound, Huxley, Beckett, Orwell, Burroughs, Gysin—all of whom succeeded in loosening social, political, religious linearities, and encouraging subjectivity and innovative reprogramming of chaotic realities.

The most influential literary work of this period was produced by James Joyce. In *Ulysses* and *Finnegans Wake*, Joyce fissioned and sliced the grammatical structure of language into thought-bytes. Joyce was not only a writer, but also a word processor, a protohacker, reducing ideas to elemental units and endlessly recombining them at will. Joyce programmed reality using his own basic language, a quantum linguistic that allowed him to assemble and reassemble thoughts into fugal, repetitious, contrapuntal patterns. It helped that he was semi-blind and dyslexic.)

Imagine what James Joyce could have done with MS Word or a CD-ROM graphic system or a modern data base! Well, we don't have to imagine—he actually managed to do it using his own brainware.

Jazz

The most effective pre-computer rendition of quantum-digital art was to be found in a certain low-life high-tech style of spontaneous, cool, subjective, improvisational sound waves produced by a small group of black audio engineers. Jazz suddenly popped up at the height of the industrial age, eroding its linear values and noninteractive styles. A factory society demands regularity, dependability, replicability, predictability, conformity. There is no room for improvisation or syncopated individuality on a Newtonian assembly line; so it was left to the African-Americans, who never really bought the factory culture, to get us boogying into the postindustrial quantum age. Needless to say, the moralists instinctively denounced jazz as chaotic, low life, and vaguely sinful.

> There is no room for improvisation or syncopated individuality on a Newtonian assembly line.

Radio

The most important factor in preparing a society of assembly-line workers and factory managers for the quantum information age was the invention of a user-friendly electronic appliance called radio.

Radio is the communication of audible signals, such as words or music, encoded in electromagnetic waves. Radio allows us to package and transmit ideas in digital patterns. The first use of "wireless" was by government, military, and business, but within one generation the home micro radio allowed the individual to turn on and tune in a range of realities.

When Farmer Jones learned how to select stations by moving the dial, he had taken the first hands-on step toward the information age. By 1936 the comforting sounds of Amos 'n' Andy and swing music had prepared human beings for the magic of quantum electronic communication, as well as the brainwashing powers of political leaders.

Movies Project Realities onto Screens

The next step in creating an electronic computer culture was a big one. Light waves passed through celluloid frames projected life like images on screens, producing new levels of reality that transformed human thought and communication.

It was a big step when computer designers decided to output data on screens instead of those old green-white Gutenberg printouts. The silent movies made this innovation possible. It is, perhaps, no accident that in the 1980s IBM used the lovable, irresistible icon of the Little Tramp in its commercials.

The next time you direct your hypnotized eyeballs toward your lit-up terminal, remember that it was cheerful Charlie Chaplin who first accustomed our species to accept the implausible quantum reality of electrical impulses flashing on a flat screen.

TV Brought the Language of Electrons into Our Homes

World War II was the first high tech war. It was fought on electronic screens: radar, sonar. The Allied victory was enormously aided by Alan Turing, the father of artificial intelligence, who used primitive computers to crack the German codes.

As soon as the war was over, these new technologies became available for civilian use. There is simply no way that a culture of television addicts can comprehend or appreciate the changes in human psychology brought about by the boob tube.

The average American spends more time per week watching television than in any other social activity. Pixels dancing on a screen are the central reality. People spend more time gazing at electrons than they do gazing into the eyes of their loved ones, looking into books, scanning other aspects of material reality. Talk about applied metaphysics! Electronic reality is more real than the physical world! This is a profound evolutionary leap. It can be compared to the jump from ocean to shoreline, when land and air suddenly become more real to the ex-fish than water!

Television Passivity

The first generation of television watching produced a nation of "vidiots"—passive amoeboids sprawled in front of the feeding-screen sucking up digital information. Giant networks controlled the airwaves, hawking commercial products and packaged politics like carnival snake oil salesmen.

Perceptive observers realized that Orwell's nightmare of a Big Brother society was too optimistic. In *1984* the authoritarian state used television to spy on citizens. The actuality is much worse: citizens docilely, voluntarily lining themselves up in front of the authority box, enjoying the lethal, neurological fast food dished out in technicolour by Newspeak.

Visionary prophets like Marshall McLuhan understood what was happening. He said, "The medium is the message." Never mind about the junk on the screen. That will change and improve. The point is that people are receiving signals on the screen. McLuhan knew that the new electronic technology would create the new global language when the time was ripe, i.e., when society had been prepared to take this quantum leap.

Computer Passivity

The first generations of computer users similarly did not understand the nature of the quantum revolution. Top management saw computers as Invaluable Business Machines[TL]. Computers simply produced higher efficiency by replacing muscular-factory-clerical labor.

And the rest of us—recognizing in the 1960s that computers in the hands of the managers would increase their power to manipulate and control us—developed a fear and loathing of computers.

Some sociologists with paranoid survival tendencies have speculated that this phobic revulsion against electronic communication shared by millions of college-educated, liberal book readers was deliberately created by Counter Intelligence Authorities[TL], whose control would be eroded by widespread electronic literacy.

The plot further thickened when countercultural code-cowgirls and code-cowboys, combining the insights and liberated attitudes of beats, hippies, acidheads, rock 'n' rollers, hackers, cyberpunks, and electronic visionaries, rode into Silicon Valley and foiled the great brain robbery by developing the great equalizer: the Personal Computer.

The birth of the information age occurred in 1976, not in a smoky industrial town like Bethlehem, PA, but in a

Freedom in any country is measured by the percentage of personal computers in the hands of individuals?

humble manger—garage—in sunny, postindustrial Silicon Valley. The Personal Computer was invented by two bearded, long-haired guys, St. Stephen the Greater and St. Steven the Lesser. And to complete the biblical metaphor, the infant prodigy was named after the Fruit of the Tree of Knowledge: the Apple! The controlled substance with which Eve committed the first original sin: Thinking for Herself!

The Personal Computer triggered a new round of confrontation in the age-old social-political competition: control by the state and individual freedom of thought. Remember how the Athenian PCs, goaded by code-cowboys like Socrates and Plato, hurled back the mainframes of the Spartans and the Persians? Remember how the moveable-type press in private hands printed out the hard copy that overthrew theocratic control of the papacy and later disseminated the Declaration of Independence? Is it not true that freedom in any country is measured perfectly by the percentage of Personal Computers in the hands of individuals?

Role of the Free Agent

Those who like to think for themselves—free agents—tend to see computers as thought-appliances. "Appliance" defines a device that individuals use in the home for their own comfort, entertainment, or education.

What are the applications of a thought-appliance? Self-improvement? Self-education. Home entertainment? Mind interplay with friends? Thought games? Mental fitness? Significant pursuits?

Free agents use their minds not to perform authorized duties for the soviet state or the International Bureaucracy Machine^{TL} but for anything that damn well suits their fancies as Americans. In the old industrial civilization you called yourself a worker, but in the information age you're a free agent. As you develop your agency, you develop your skills in communication.

Personal Computer Owners are Discovering That the Brain is:

•◆ The ultimate organ for pleasure and awareness;

•◆ An array of a hundred billion micro-computers waiting to be booted up, activated, stimulated, and programmed;

•◆ Waiting impatiently for software, headware, thoughtware that pays respect to its awesome potential and makes possible electronic internet linkage with other brains.

12

FROM YIPPIES TO YUPPIES

Before 1946, youngsters absorbed and joined their culture by means of personal observation of significant grown ups. You watched the neighborhood doctor and the local carpenter and the nurse or the maiden aunt, and you drifted into a job. Books, sermons, magazine articles about heroic or antisocial figures also helped define the nature of the social game.

Television changed all that. The average American household watches television more than seven hours a day. This statistic means that yuppies learned about culture, absorbed the roles, rules, rituals, styles, and jargon of the game, not from personal observation but from television images. The cartoons, soap operas, prime time dramas, and game shows tend to be escapist. The news broadcasts tend to feature victims and righteous whiners rather than successful role models. Politicians reciting rehearsed lies are not seen as credible heroes.

The only aspect of television that presents real people engaged in actions that are existen-

tially true, credible, and scientifically objective
are the sportscasts. This may explain the enormous media attention given to organized athlet-
ics. The average kid watches Fernando Valen-
zuela or Joe Montana or Kareem Abdul Jabbar
perform and is then exposed to endless interviews
with and stories about these successful, self-made
professionals. Their opinions, moods, physical ail-
ments, philosophies, and lifestyles are presented
in microscopic detail. People know more about
Larry Bird as a "real person" than they do about
Walter Mondale or George Bush or Dan Rather.

Any predictions about the future that the
yuppies created was based on the fact that they
were the first members of the information communication culture. It is inevitable that they
would become more realistic, more professional,
more skilled. Intelligence was their ethos and
their model. They understand that the smart
thing to do was to construct a peaceful, fair, just,
compassionate social order.

Enter Yuppies

After my deportation from Harvard
University many years ago, I was, among
other things, a freelance college professor paid
by students for one-night-stand lectures about
topics too hot for salaried professors.

Back in the Sixties when I flew in for a lecture, the student committee showed up at the
airport wearing long hair, sandals, blue jeans,
and cheerful, impudent grins. The radio would
be blasting out Mick Jagger and Jimi Hendrix
as we drove to the campus. The students eagerly

asked me about "high" technologies—methods of consciousness expansion, new brands of wonder drugs, new forms of protest, up-to-date developments in the ever-changing metaphysical philosophies of rock stars: Yoko Ono's theory of astrology; Peter Townsend's devotion to Baba Ram Dass. I kept abreast of these subjects and tried to give responsive answers.

That all changed. The lecture committee arrived at the airport wearing three piece suits, briefcases, clipboards with schedules. No music. No questions about Michael Jackson's theory of reincarnation or Sheena Easton's concept of sugar walls. The impudent grins were gone. The young people were cool, realistic, and corporate-minded. They questioned me about computer stocks, electronic books, and prospects for careers in software.

Anatomy of a Yuppie

The moralists of both left and right can froth with righteous indignation about this army of selfish, career-oriented, entrepreneurial individualists who apparently value money and their own interests more than the lofty causes of yesteryear. But behind the trendy hype, we sense that the twitchy media may be reflecting some authentic change in the public consciousness.

**The phrase "young urban professionals" didn't tell us much.
I guess the implication was that they were not old rural amateurs—ORAs. But who were they?**

The yuppie myth expressed a vague sense that something different, something not yet understood but possibly meaningful, was happening in the day-to-day lives and dreams of young people growing up in this very unsettling world.

Surely it's important to understand what was going on with this most influential group of human beings on the planet—the 76 million materialistic, educated or streetwise, performance-driven Americans becoming adults in the latter 20th Century.

 ## Yuppies were a new breed

This much we know: The yuppies were a new breed. They were the first members of the electronic society. They were the first crop of bewildered mutants climbing out of the muck of the industrial—late neolithic smokestack—age. They showed up on the scene in 1946, a watershed year, marking the end of World War II—the war that induced the birth of electronic technology: radar, sonar, atomic fission, computers. In 1946, this incredible high-tech gear was beginning to be available for civilian consumption.

Something else important happened in 1946. The birthrate in America unexpectedly doubled. Between 1946 and 1964, 76 million babies were born. That's 40 million more than demographers predicted. These postwar kids were the first members of a new species: *Homo sapiens electronicus.* From the time they could peer out of the crib, they were exposed to a constant shower of information beaming from screens.

They were, right from the start, treated like no other generation in human history. Their parents raised them according to Dr. Benjamin Spock's totally revolutionary theory of child care. "Treat your kids as individuals," said Spock. "Tell them that they are special! Tell them to think for themselves. Feed them, not according to some factory schedule. Feed them on gourmet demand, i.e., let 'em eat what they want when they are hungry."

Postwar kids were the first members of a new species, Homo sapiens electronicus. From the time they could peer out of the crib, they were exposed to a constant shower of information beaming from screens.

This generation is the most intelligent group of human beings ever to inhabit the planet. The best educated. The most widely traveled. The most sophisticated. They have grew up adapting to an accelerated rate of change that is almost incomprehensible. They became highly selective consumers, expecting to be rewarded because they are the best.

Let's hasten to clear up one misconception here. This postwar generation of Spockies was not docilely manipulated by greedy ad men or the cynical media. Nor was it the so called image makers, the rock stars and television programmers and moviemakers, telling the kids what to do. Quite to the contrary. The Spockies themselves dictated to the imageers and marketeers about what they wanted.

Baby-Boomers Grow Up

The rapidly changing style and tone of American culture in the second half of the 20th Century has reflected the elitist expectations of this Spock generation as it passed through the normal stages of maturation.

During the 1950s, kids were clean cut and easygoing. The tumultuous Sixties marked the stormy adolescence of this astonishing generation and bore the hippies—bands of cheerful, muddling sensualists and self-proclaimed dropouts. By the 1970s, Spockies were busy stopping the Vietnam War, peaceably overthrowing the Nixon administration, and mainly trying to figure out what to do with their lives. The Eighties brought us a new breed of individualists turned professional.

The Fifties are fondly remembered as the child-centered, home-based decade. Popular music, being most free from parental control, provided the clearest expression of youthful mood. The first stirrings of adolescence changed the beat. Spockies wanted to wiggle their hips tentatively; so the hula-hoop craze swept the land. The music picked up the beat with rhythm 'n' blues, rockabilly, rock 'n' roll, the Surfer and the Motown sound. Just as cute, fuzzy caterpillars suddenly metamorphose into gaudy butterflies, so did the sweet, cuddly Mouseketeers moult into high-flying, highly visible, highly vulnerable hippies.

The Spockies emerging into teenage pubescence in the 1960s changed our traditional notions about sex, duty, work, conformity, and sacrifice. The postwar kids never really accepted the values of the industrial society or the aesthetics of the Depression era. They never bought the Protestant work ethic. After watching television six hours a day for fifteen years, would they settle docilely for a hard hat job on the assembly line?

Bob Dylan set the tone for the adolescent rebellion: "Don't follow leaders. Watch your parking meters." The Beach Boys offered a California style of personal freedom. The Beatles picked up the theme of bouncy irreverence. It seemed so natural. All you need is love. Do your own thing.

The Sixties were unflurried, unworried, more erotic than neurotic. We're not gonna be wage slaves or fight the old men's wars. We're all gonna live in a yellow submarine!

It wasn't just middle class white males calling for changes. The blacks were ready. They had been waiting four hundred years. The race riots and the civil-rights protests and the freedom marches were an unexpected fallout of Spockian philosophy. It is hard to overestimate the effect of the black culture on the Spockie generation. There was the music, of course. The style, the grace, the coolness, the cynical Zen detachment from the system came from the blacks. No white professor had to tell the blacks to turn on, tune in, and drop out of conformity.

Then there was the women's liberation movement, perhaps the most significant change impulse of the century. This was the smartest, best-educated group of women in history, and they expected to be treated as individuals. And the gay-pride concept was stirring. Apparently their parents had read Spock, too. Not since the democratic, human-rights movements of the 18th Century had there been so much feverish hope for a fair and free social order.

But by the end of the decade it became apparent that utopia wasn't going to happen that easily.

Why Utopia Isn't Going to Happen

1. There were powerful forces dead-set against any change in American culture.

2. There were no practical blueprints or role models for harnessing a vague philosophy of individualism into a functioning social order.

3. Basically, we were not quite ready: The Spockies were still kids outnumbered demographically and unprepared psychologically to create the postindustrial phase of human culture.

The opposition to change had made itself very apparent in the cold-blooded assassinations of Jack Kennedy, brother Bobby, Malcolm X, and Martin Luther King, Jr. Lyndon Johnson, Richard Nixon, and the new cowboy governor of California made it perfectly clear that they would happily use force to protect their system.

The social philosophy of the hippies was romantically impractical. Sure, they weren't gonna work on Maggie's farm no more, but what were they gonna do after bailing all night long? Some retreated to gurus, others went back to a new form of anti-technological chic Amishness. Urban political activists parroted slogans of European or third-world socialism and made pop stars of totalitarian leaders like Che Guevara and Ho Chi Minh. The debacle at Altamont and the conjunction of overdose deaths of rock stars Joplin, Hendrix, and Morrison symbolized the end of the Sixties.

The Next Phase

By the end of the Sixties, many young people had lost confidence in the old establishments. The phrase "Don't trust anyone over 30" reflected a disillusioned realism; you couldn't find answers in the grand ol' GOP or the Democratic party. Big business and big labor were both unresponsive to the obvious need for change; the high ideals of socialism seemed to translate into just another word for police-state bureaucracy. By the end of the decade, it was also clear to any sensible young person that individualism and doing your own thing had a certain drawback. If you weren't gonna work for Maggie's pa no more, how were you gonna make out?

The obvious answer: You were gonna believe in yourself. That's what the Seventies were all about. More than 76 million Spockies reached the venerable age of 24 and faced a very practical challenge: Grow up!

The focus became self-improvement, EST,

Those who think for themselves—free agents—tend to see computers as thought-appliances.

assertiveness training, personal excellence, career planning. Tom Wolfe, always the shrewd social critic, coined the term "the me generation."

Then a recession hit. Arab-oil blackmail pushed up inflation rates. Adult society had no expansion-growth plans to harness the energies of 40 million extra people. Indeed, growing automation was reducing the work force. The Iran hostage crisis lowered morale. In the malaise, the voters chose the smiling Ronald Reagan over a frustrated Carter. The Spockies boycotted the election.

Most young Americans today don't want to be forced to work at jobs that can be done better by machines. They don't want to stand on assembly lines repeating mindless tasks. Robots work. Citizens in socialist workers' countries work. Grizzled veterans in the steel towns of Pennsylvania work. Third-world people have to work to survive.

What do self-respecting, intelligent, ambitious young Americans do? They perform. They master a craft. They learn to excel in a personal skill. They become entrepreneurs, i.e., people who organize, operate, and assume risks. They employ themselves, they train themselves, they promote themselves, they transfer themselves, they reward themselves.

They perform exactly those functions that can't be done by CAD-CAM machines, however precisely programmed. They gravitate naturally to postindustrial fields-electronics, communication, education, merchandising, marketing, entertainment, skilled personal service, health and growth enterprises, leisure-time professions.

They are politically and psychologically independent. They do not identify with company or union or partisan party. They do not depend on organizational tenure. They are notoriously non-loyal to institutions.

Cyberpunks are the inventors, innovative writers, techno-frontier artists, risk-taking film directors, icon-shifting composers, stand-up comedians, expressionist artists, free-agent scientists, techno-creatives, computer visionaries, elegant hackers, bit-blithng Prolog adepts, special-effectives, cognitive dissidents, video wizards, neurological test pilots, media explorers— all of those who boldly package and steer ideas out there where no thoughts have gone before.

13

CYBERPUNKS

Cyber means "pilot." A "Cyberperson" is one who pilots his/her own life. By definition, the cyberperson is fascinated by navigational information—especially maps, charts, labels, guides, manuals that help pilot one through life. The cyberperson continually searches for theories, models, paradigms, metaphors, images, icons that help chart and define the realities that we inhabit.

"Cybertech" refers to the tools, appliances, and methodologies of knowing and communicating. Linguistics. Philosophy. Semantics. Semiotics. Practical epistemologies. The ontologies of daily life. Words, icons, pencils, printing presses, screens, keyboards, computers, disks.

"Cyberpolitics" introduces the Foucault notions of the use of language and linguistic-tech by the ruling classes in feudal and industrial societies to control children, the uneducated, and the under classes. The words "governor" or "steersman" or "G-man" are used to describe those who manipulate words and communication devices in order to control, to bolster authority—

feudal, management, government—and to discourage innovative thought and free exchange.

Cyberpunks use all available data-input to think for themselves. You know who they are. Every stage of history has produced names and heroic legends for the strong, stubborn, creative individuals who explore some future frontier, collect and bring back new information, and offer to guide the human gene pool to the next stage. Typically, these time mavericks combine bravery, and high curiosity, with super self-esteem. These three characteristics are considered necessary for those engaged in the profession of genetic guide, aka counterculture philosopher.

The classical Olde Westworld model for the cyberpunk is Prometheus, a technological genius who "stole" lire from the Gods and gave it to humanity. Prometheus also taught his gene pool many useful arts and sciences. According to the official version of the legend, he/she was exiled from the gene pool and sentenced to the ultimate torture for these unauthorized transmissions of classified information. In another version of the myth (unauthorized), Prometheus (aka the Pied Piper) uses his/her skills to escape the sinking kinship taking with him/her the cream of the gene pool.

> **The classical Olde Westworld model for the cyberpunk is Prometheus, a technological genius who "stole" lire from the Gods and gave it to humanity.**

The Newe World version of this ancient myth is Quetzalcoatl, God of civilization, high-tech wizard who introduced maize, the calendar, erotic sculpture, flute-playing, the arts, and the sciences. He was driven into exile by the G-man in power, who was called Tezcathpoca.

Self-assured singularities of the cyberbreed have been called mavericks, ronin, freelancers, independents, self-starters, nonconformists, oddballs, troublemakers, kooks, visionaries, iconoclasts, insurgents, blue-sky thinkers, loners, smart alecks. Before Gorbachev, the Soviets scornfully called them hooligans. Religious organizations have always called them heretics. Bureaucrats call them disloyal dissidents, traitors, or worse. In the old days, even sensible people called them mad.

They have been variously labeled clever, creative, entrepreneurial, imaginative, enterprising, fertile, ingenious, inventive, resourceful, talented, eccentric.

During the tribal, feudal, and industrial-literate phrases of human evolution, the logical survival traits were conformity and dependability. The "good serf" or "vassal" was obedient. The "good worker" or "manager" was reliable. Maverick thinkers were tolerated only at moments when innovation and change were necessary, usually to deal with the local competition.

In the information communication civilization of the 21st Century, creativity and mental excellence will become the ethical norm. The world will be too dynamic, complex, and diversified, too cross-linked by the global immediacies of modern—quantum—communication, for stability of thought or dependability of behavior to be successful. The "good persons" in the cy-

Cyberpunks use all available data-input to quesiton authority andthink for themselves

bernetic society are the intelligent ones who can think for themselves. The "problem person" in the cybernetic society of the 21st Century is the one who automatically obeys, who never, questions authority, who acts to protect his/her official status, who placates and politics rather than thinks independently.

Thoughtful Japanese are worried about the need for ronin thinking in their obedient culture, the postwar generation now taking over.

Greek Word for "Pilot"

The term "cybernetics" comes from the Greek word *kubernetes*, "pilot"

The Hellenic origin of this word is important in that it reflects the Socratic-Platonic traditions of independence and individual self-reliance which, we are told, derived from geography. The proud little Greek city-states were perched on peninsular fingers wiggling down into the fertile Mediterranean Sea, protected by mountains from the land-mass armies of Asia.

Mariners of those ancient days had to be bold and resourceful. Sailing the seven seas without maps or navigational equipment, they were forced to develop independence of thought The self-reliance that these Hellenic pilots developed in their voyages probably carried over to the democratic, inquiring, questioning nature of their land life.

The Athenian cyberpunks, the pilots, made their own navigational decisions.

These psychogeographical factors may have contributed to the humanism of the Hellenic religions that emphasized freedom, pagan joy, celebration of life, and speculative thought. The humanist and polytheistic religions of ancient Greece are often compared with the austere morality of monotheistic Judaism, the fierce, dogmatic polarities of Persian-Arab dogma, and the imperial authority of Roman—Christian—culture.

Roman Concept of Director, Governor, Steersman

The Greek word *kubernetes*, when translated to Latin, comes out as *gubernetes*. This basic verb gubernare means to control the actions or behavior, to direct, to exercise sovereign authority, to regulate, to keep under, to restrain, to steer. This Roman concept is obviously very different from the Hellenic notion of "pilot"

It maybe relevant that the Latin term "to steer" comes from the word stare, which means "to stand," with derivative meanings "place or thing which is standing." The past participle of the Latin word produces "status," "state," "institute," "statue," "static," "statistics," "prostitute," "restitute," "constitute."

The word "cybernetics" was coined in 1948 by Norbert Weiner, who wrote, "we have decided to call the entire field of control and communication theory, whether in the machine or in the animal, by the name of Cybernetics, which we form from the Greek for steersman. [sic]"

The word "cyber" has been redefined in the American Heritage Dictionary as "the theoretical study of control processes in electronic, mechanical, and biological systems, especially the flow of information in such systems." The derivative word "cybernate" means "to control automatically by computer or to be so controlled."

An even more ominous interpretation defines cybernetics as "the study of human control mechanisms and their replacement by mechanical or electronic systems."

Note how Weiner and the Romanesque engineers have corrupted the meaning of "cyber." The Greek word "pilot" becomes "governor" or "director"; the term "to steer" becomes "to control."

Now we are liberating the term, teasing it free from serfdom to represent the autopoetic, self-directed principle of organization that arises in the universe in many systems of widely varying sizes, in people, societies, and atoms.

Politics of Literacy

The etymological distinctions between Greek and Roman terms are quite relevant to the pragmatics of the culture surrounding their usage. French philosophy, for example, has recently stressed the importance of language and semiotics in determining human behavior and social structures. Michel Foucault's classic studies of linguistic politics and mind control led him to believe

that human consciousness—as expressed
in speech and images, in self-definition

and mutual designation is the authentic locale of the determinant politics of being.... What men and women are born into is only superficially this or that social, legislative, and executive system. Their ambiguous, oppressive birthright is the language, the conceptual categories, the conventions of identification and perception, which have evolved and, very largely, atrophied up to the time of their personal and social existence. It is the established but customarily subconscious, unargued constraints of awareness that enslave.

To remove the means of expressing dissent is to remove the possibility of dissent.

Orwell and Wittgenstein and McLuhan agree. To remove the means of expressing dissent is to remove the possibility of dissent. "Whereof one cannot speak, thereof must one remain silent." In this light the difference between the Greek word "pilot" and the Roman translation "governor" becomes a most significant semantic manipulation, and the flexibility granted to symbol systems of all kinds by their representation in digital computers becomes dramatically liberating.

Do we pride ourselves for becoming ingenious "pilots" or dutiful "controllers"?

What is Governetics?

The word "governetics" refers to an attitude of obedience-control in relationship to self or others. Pilots, those who navigate on the seven seas or in the sky, have to devise and execute course changes continually in response to the changing environment. They respond continually to feedback, information about the environment. Dynamic. Alert. Alive.

The Latinate "steersman," by contrast, is in the situation of following orders. The Romans, we recall, were great organizers, road-builders, administrators. The galleys, the chariots must be controlled. The legions of soldiers must be directed.

The Hellenic concept of the individual navigating his/her own course was an island of humanism in a raging sea of totalitarian empires. To the East—the past—were the centralized, authoritarian kingdoms. The governors of Iran, from Cyrus, the Persian emperor, to the recent shah and ayatollah, have exemplified the highest traditions of state control.

The Greeks were flanked on the other side, which we shall designate as the West—or future, by a certain heavy concept called Rome. The caesars and popes of the Holy Roman Empire represented the next grand phase of institutional control. The governing hand on the wheel stands for stability, durability, continuity, permanence. Staying the course. Individual creativity, exploration, and change are usually not encouraged.

Pilots of the Species

The terms "cybernetic person" or "cybernaut" return us to the original meaning of "pilot" and puts the self reliant person back in the loop. These words—and the more pop term "cyberpunk"—refer to the personalization—and thus the popularization—of knowledge-information technology, to innovative thinking on the part of the individual.

According to McLuhan and Foucault, if you change the language, you change the society. Following their lead, we suggest that the terms "cybernetic person, cybernaut" may describe a new species model of human being and a new social order. "Cyberpunk" is, admittedly, a risky term. Like all linguistic innovations, it must be used with a tolerant sense of high-tech humor. It's a stopgap, transitional meaning-grenade thrown over the language barricades to describe the resourceful, skillful individual who accesses and steers knowledge-communication technology toward his/her own private goals, for personal pleasure, profit, principle, or growth.

Cyberpunks are the inventors, innovative writers, techno-frontier artists, risk-taking film directors, icon-shifting composers, stand-up comedians, expressionist artists, free-agent scientists, techno-creatives, computer visionaries, elegant hackers, bit-blithng Prolog adepts, special-effectives, cognitive dissidents, video wizards, neurological test pilots, media explorers—all of those who boldly package and steer ideas out there where no thoughts have gone before.

This free-speech/free-thought movement emerges routinely when enough young people have access to electronic technology.

Countercultures are sometimes tolerated by the governors. They can, with sweet cynicism and patient humor, interface their singularity with institutions. They often work within the "governing systems" on a temporary basis. As often as not, they are unauthorized.

The "good persons" in the cybernetic society are the intelligent ones who think for themselves. The "problem persons" in the cybernetic society of the 21st Century are those who automatically obey, who never question authority, who act to protect their official status, who placate and politic rather than thinking independently.

Legend of the Ronin

Ronin is used by Beverly Potter as a metaphor based on a Japanese word for lordless samurai. As early as the 8th Century, ronin was translated literally as "wave people" and used in Japan to describe those who had left their allotted, caste-predetermined stations in life: samurai who left the service of their feudal lords to become masterless.

Ronin played a key role in Japan's abrupt transition from a feudal society to industrialism. Under feudal rule, warriors were not allowed to think freely, or act according to their will. On the other hand, having been forced by circumstances to develop independence, ronin took more readily to new ideas and technology and became increasingly influential in the independent schools.

—Beverly Potter
The Way of the Ronin

The West has many historical parallels to the ronin archetype. The term "free lance" has its origin in the period after the Crusades, when a large number of knights were separated from their lords. Many lived by the code of chivalry and became "lances for hire." The American frontier was fertile ground for the ronin archetype. "Maverick," derived from the Texan word for unbranded steer, was used to describe a free and self-directed individual.

Although many of the ronin's roots ... are in the male culture, most career women are well acquainted with the way of the ronin. Career women left their traditional stations and battled their way into the recesses of the male dominated workplaces.... Like the ronin who had no clan, professional women often feel excluded from the corporate cliques' inside tracks, without ally or mentor.

—Beverly Potter
The Way of the Ronin

Role Model for 21st Century

The tradition of the "individual who thinks for him/herself" extends to the beginnings of recorded human history. Indeed, the very label of our species, Homo sapiens, defines us as the animal who thinks.

If our genetic function is computare—to think, then it follows that the ages and stages of human history, so far, have been larval or preparatory. After the insectoid phases of submission to gene pools, the mature stage of the human life cycle is the individual who thinks for him/herself. Now at the beginnings of the information age, are we ready to assume our genetic function?

The beats stood for the ecstatic vision and for individual freedom in revolt against all bureaucratic, closed-minded systems. They saw themselves as citizens of the world. They met with Russian poets to denounce the Cold War. They practiced oriental yoga. They experimented, as artists have for centuries, with mind-opening foods and drugs and sexual practices.

14

A NEW BREED

I t had finally happened: the inevitable and
long-awaited climax of the youth revolutions.
"They aren't going to work on Brezhnev's farm
no more." The Dr. Spock-memes of self-direction
has swept the world in less than three decades.

This is not a political revolution; it's more
like a cultural evolution. A tsunami of electronic
information. The emergence of a new breed.
Young people all over the world are mutated, as
Marshall McLuhan predicted, by highly communicable memes: documentary footage, rock 'n'
roll music, MTV pirate broadcasts, all coming
to them through American-Japanese television
screens. This new breed is centered on self-direction and individual choice, a genetic revulsion
for partisan politics, a species horror of centralized governments.

This global youth movement cannot be dis-
cussed in the terms of politics or sociology or
psychology. We are dealing with a new, post-Dar-
winian, genetic science.

This emergence of youth power has been called sociogenetics, cybernetic evolution, cultural genetics, memetics. It has to do with the communication and transmission of new ideas and attitudes. Dawkins has suggested the word "memes" to describe these self-replicating ideas that sweep across human populations, bringing about cultural mutations.

Memes: Self-replicating ideas that sweep across human populations, bringing about cultural mutations.

Neoteny: (1) attainment of improved functional maturity during the larval stage; (2) retention of survivally optimal larval or immature characters as adults, i.e., refusal to stop growing, extension of the developmental period.

At the end of the 20th Century, we witnessed a new breed emerging during the juvenile stage of industrial-age society. The key word here is juvenile, as opposed to adult. Adult is the past participle of the verb "to grow." This new breed appeared when enormous numbers of individuals in the juvenile stage began intercommunicating some new memes, mutating together at the same time. The Japanese brand of this youth movement call themselves Ho Ko Ten—"the new society."

Biological evolution works through the competitive spread of genes. Logically, the mechanism of cultural change involves communication.

Individuals are activated to change when they pick up new meme-signals from others of their cohort The mode of communication determines not just the speed of the change, but the nature of the change.

Medium is the Message in the Cultural Evolution

The Ten Commandments, chiseled on stone tablets, created a fundamentalist culture that discouraged change and democratic participation. There is one God, the author-creator, and his words are eternally true. This stone—tablet meme—carrier spawns a culture ruled by the inerrant "good book" and a priest-hood of those who preserve, interpret, and en-force the commandments.

The printing press mass-disseminates memes that create a factory culture run by managers.

The electronic, McLuhanesque meme-signals that produced Woodstock nation and the Berlin Wall deconstruction are more a matter of atti-tude and style.

The television news has trained us to rec-ognize "the robe-memes"— the feudal pope—or Iranian mullah—and his solemn piety-reek-ing priests. We recognize "the suits", the adult politicians of the industrial age, with their no-nonsense sobriety. We observe "the uniforms", armed, booted, helmeted.

And since the Sixties, we have observed this new breed, "the students" who tend to wear blue jeans and running shoes. Their dress and ges-tural signals are as important as the identifying markings and scents of different species of mammals. Just like any new breed of mammals, these kids recognize each other across national boundaries. The faces of the Chinese youth shine with that same glow as the faces photographically captured in Berlin and Prague and—twenty years previously—in Woodstock.

Prime-Time Authoritarianism

It is important to note that these students are not demonstrating for "socialist democracy" or "capitalist democracy." They are for "individual freedom". In the cybernetic age, "democracy" becomes majority-mob rule and the enemy of individual freedom.

Democracy works just fine in a preindustrial, oral society in which the men walk or ride horses to the village center and talk things over. Industrial societies produce a factory system of politics run by managers. Representative government involves full-time professional politicians and partisan parties. The dismal results are predictable.

As soon as cybernetic communication appliances emerged, political power was seized by those who control the airwaves. We've seen this since the rise of fascism and totalitarianism. American elections in the Eighties produced an ominous demonstration of tele-democracy in a centralized country.

Less than 50 percent of the eligible voters bothered to register or vote in these three presidential elections. More than half of adult Americans were so disillusioned, apathetic, bored that they made the intelligent decision to vote, in absentia, for "none of the above." According to exit polls, more than half of voting Americans glumly admitted that they were choosing "the lesser of two evils."

Republican presidents in the Eighties were elected by around 25 percent of the citizenry. The only ones who really cared about these elections were those who stood to benefit financially from the results. The "apparatchiks" and government-payrolled "nomenclatura" of the two contending "parties" choose the "leaders" who would preside over division of the spoils.

History will note that the Eighties Republican mirrored the Brezhnevian anomie in the Soviet Union. It is now shockingly clear that the Republican party in this country plays the role of the Communist party in the pre-Gorbachev USSR: an entrenched, conservative, militaristic, unashamedly corrupt, secretive, belligerently nationalistic bureaucracy. It gave the country twelve years of stagnation, spiritless boredom, and cynical greed.

Meanwhile, the all-star huckster of freedom and decentralization, Mikhail Gorbachev, in five remarkable years persuaded an entire subcontinent to "drop out" of Stalinism.

In this climate it is obvious that the party apparatus with the biggest budget for television advertising and the marketing ability to focus on the most telegenic, shallow, flamboyantly lurid issues (abortion, drugs, pledge of allegiance, school prayer, no taxes, and jingoistic, bellicose nationalism) would sweep to a landslide win on the votes of the 25 percent majority.

This new breed is centered on self-direction and individual choice, a genetic revulsion for partisan politics, a species horror of centralized governments.

It is ironic that in the oldest democracy, the U.S., partisan politics seems to have lost touch with reality. In the elections of the Eighties, millions were expended on political advertising. Elections were won by paid-time commercials involving moralistic images, emotional theatrics, and malicious fabrications. Old-fashioned religious demonology and fake patriotism, skillfully splashed across the television screens, replaced rational discussion of issues.

End of Majoritarian Democracy

In the feudal and industrial ages, majoritarian democracy was usually a powerful libertarian counterculture force defending the individual against regal tyranny and class slavery. In the early years of the electronic-information stage (1950-1990), the ability of the religious-industrial-military rulers to manipulate television converted town hall democracy into majoritarian, prime-time, sit-corn totalitarianism.

Cybernetic media in the hands of politicians with shockingly large advertising budgets plays to the dread LCD—lowest common denominator. The new fragile democracies in eastern Europe will probably have to pass through this phase of marketeer, televoid elections manipulated by "spin doctors" and dishonest advertising.

So much for the down side. The good news is that cybernetic media cannot be controlled. Electronic signals flashing around the atmosphere cannot be kept out by stone walls or border police dogs. Japanese tape-decks, ghetto-blasters, digital appliances in the hands of the individual empowers the HCD—highest common denominator.

Sociology of Quantum Physics

The philosophy that predicted this movement is not capitalism or socialism. It is not industrial democracy—the tyranny of the 25 percent majority. Psychedelic concepts like glasnost and perestroika are based on the common-sense principles of quantum physics—relativity, flexibility, singularity.

Werner Heisenberg's equations described the fabrication of singular, personal realities based on free, open communication. Objective indeterminacy, that bane of the mechanical mind, means individual determinism and self-reliance—the mottoes of the new breed.

Dr. Spock Personalizes Quantum Psychology

In 1946, quantum physics was translated into common-sense, hands-on psychology by a pediatrician. The youth movement was generated by a genial child psychologist who taught two generations of postwar parents to feed their children on demand. "Treat your kids as individuals, as singularities." Here was the most radical, subversive social doctrine ever proposed, and it was directed to the only groups that can bring about enduring change: parents, pediatricians, teachers.

This postwar generation of indulged, "self-centered" individuals started to appear exactly when the new psychedelic-cybernetic brain change technologies became available to individuals.

McLuhan Empowers Quantum Psychology

The babyboomers were the first television species, the first human beings who used electronic digital appliances to turn on and tune in realities; the first to use neurotransmitting chemicals to change their own brains; the first members of this "global village" made possible by television.

The fall of the Berlin Wall was accomplished by youth seeking individual freedom. This student counterculture started in America in the 1960s, and it was spread via electronic media.

"Hongk is all the rage in the Mongolian People's Republic. It's a key part of the Shineshiel (perestroika) that has been sweeping the remote communist nation for weeks now.... Hongk is the name of the rock 'n' roll band that has been playing its powerful, dissident songs to packed audiences in the state owned auditoriums of Mongolia's capitol of Ulan Bator for months now. Its music has become the unchallenged anthem of the city's fledgling protest movement" (*Los Angeles Times*).

Function of Post-Democratic Government

The primary function of a free society in the post-democratic age is the protection of individual freedom from politicians who attempt to limit personal freedom.

This individual-freedom movement is new to human history, because it is not based on geography, politics, class, or religion. It has to do with changes, not in the power structure, not in who controls the police, but in the individual's mind. It is a "head" revolution: a consciousness-raising affair. It involves "thinking for yourself." This cultural meme involves intelligence, personal access to information, an anti-ideological reliance on common sense, mental proficiency, consciousness raising, street smarts, intelligent consumerism-hedonism, personal-communication skills. The meme-idea is not new. Countercultures go back at least as far as Hermes Trismegistus, and include Socrates, Paracelsus, the Renaissance, Voltaire, Emerson, Thoreau, Dada, Gurdjieff, and Crowley.

But the rapid spread of this mutational meme from 1960 to 1990 was due to the sudden, mass availability of neurochemical and electronic technology. Demand feeding. Chemicals and screens spraying electronic information into eye drums and ear balls, activating brains. Suddenly, youth all over the world are wearing

J.F.K. was a memetic agent, literally creating a new breed!

jeans and listening to John Lennon's "Give Peace a Chance." The individuality meme that swept American youth during the Sixties has infected the world.

In the Seventies, the Spock-McLuhan epidemic spread around western Europe. The signs of this awakening are always the same. Young minds exposed to the free spray of electronic information suddenly blossom like flowers in the spring. The June 1989 demonstrations in Tien An Men square were a classic replay of Chicago 1968 and Kent State 1970.

Power, Mao said, comes from the barrel of a gun. That may have been true in the industrial past, but in cybernetic Ninties, the very notion of political "power" seems anachronistic, kinky, sick. For the new breed the notion of "political power" is hateful, evil, ghastly. The idea that any group should want to grab domination, control, authority, supremacy, or jurisdiction over others is a primitive perversity—as loathsome and outdated as slavery or cannibalism.

It was not the Berlin Wall of concrete and guard houses that protected the "evil empire"; it was the electronic wall that was easily breached by MTV. McLuhan and Foucault have demonstrated that freedom depends upon who controls the technologies that reach your brain-telephones, the editing facility, the neurochemicals, the screen.

Mass Individualism is New

This sudden emergence of humanism and open-mindedness on a mass scale is new.

In tribal societies the role of the individual is to be a submissive, obedient child. The tribal elders do the thinking. Survival pressures do not afford them the luxury of freedom.

In feudal societies the individual is a serf or vassal, peasant, chattel, peon, slave. The nobles and priests do the thinking. They are trained by tradition to abhor and anathematize open mindedness and thinking for yourself.

This sudden emergence of humanism and open-mindedness on a mass scale is new.

After the tribal—familial—arid feudal—childlike—stages of human evolution came the industrial—insectoid—society, where the individual is a worker or manager, in later stages, a worker-consumer.

In all these static, primitive societies, the thinking is done by the organizations who control the guns. The power of open-minded individuals to make and remake decisions about their own lives, to fabricate, concoct, invent, prevaricate their own lies is severely limited. Youth had no power, no voice, no choice.

The post-political information society; which we are now developing, does not operate on the basis of obedience and conformity to dogma. It is based on individual thinking, scientific know-how, quick exchange of facts around feedback networks, high tech ingenuity, and practical, front-line creativity. The society of the future no longer grudgingly tolerates a few open minded innovators. The cybernetic society is totally dependent on a large pool of such people, communicating at light speed with each other across state lines and national boundaries. Electrified

The postwar generation of indulged, "self-centered" individuals appeared when the new psychedelic-cybernetic brain change technologies became available to individuals.

thoughts invite fast feedback, creating new global societies that require a higher level of electronic know how, psychological sophistication, and open minded intelligence.

This cyber communication process is accelerating so rapidly that to compete on the world information market of the 21st Century, nations, companies, even families must be composed of change-oriented, innovative individuals who are adepts in communicating via the new cyber electronic technologies.

The new breeds are simply much smarter than the old guard. They inhale new information the way they breathe oxygen. They stimulate each other to continually upgrade and reformat their minds. People who use cyber technology to make fast decisions on their jobs are not going to go home and passively let aging, closed-minded white, male politicians make decisions about their lives.

The emergence of this new open-minded caste in different countries around the world is the central historical issue of the last fifty years.

The Revolutions Began with the Beats

In the Fifties in America, at the height of the television Cold War, there appeared a group of free people who created highly communicable counterculture memes that were to change history. The beats stood for the ecstatic vision and for individual freedom in revolt against all bureaucratic, dosed minded systems. They saw themselves as citizens of the world. They met with Russian poets to denounce the Cold War. They practiced oriental yoga. They experimented, as artists have for centuries, with mind opening foods and drugs and sexual practices.

Most important, with their minds turning like satellite dishes to other cultures, they had an historical sense of what they were doing. They saw themselves as heirs to the long tradition of intellectual and artistic individualism that goes beyond national boundaries.

What made the beats more effective than any dissident-artist group in human history was the timing. Electronic technology made it possible for their bohemian memes, their images, and their sounds to be broadcast at almost the speed of light around the world. Just as soap companies were using television and radio to market their products, so the beats used the electronic media to advertise their ideas. The hippie culture of the Sixties and the liberation movements in Eastern Europe are indebted to the libertarian dissenting of the 'fifties counterculture.

Bringing the Sixties to China

The Be-In in San Francisco in January of 1967 produced an ocean of youth who gathered to celebrate their beings and their solidarity. It turned out to be the dawning of the psychedelic-cybernetic age—or glasnost, as it is now called. The San Francisco Be-In was

not organized. The word got out via the underground press, progressive radio stations, word
of mouth. Three months later the International
Monterey Pop festival harnessed the flourishing
psychedelic spirit to electrically amplified music.

The symbol of the counterculture was the
widely repeated image of a young man putting a
flower in the gun barrel of the National Guards-
man who was threatening him. The students in
Tien An Men Square in June 1989 remembered.
Their stated purpose was to bring the Sixties to
China. The epidemic of freedom-memes in China
caught the authorities totally off guard—just
like the numbers at the Woodstock festival.

Self-Government

Partisan politics is over. In the post-political age,
people are catching on to the bottom-line fact: The
only function of a political party is to keep itself in office.

This free-speech/free-thought movement
emerges routinely when enough young people
have access to electronic technology. When the
rulers of China made telephones and television
sets available to millions of people, the swarming of activated youth in Tien An Men Square
was guaranteed. Many of the Chinese students
had seen television coverage of student demonstrations in other countries. When East German
television stations began transmitting programs
from the West, the Berlin Wall was on its way
down. In each nation, the free-thought movement of the Eighties was produced by students
and intellectuals who learned how to use electronic
appliances and digital computers to think for

themselves, fabricate their personal mythologies, and communicate their irreverent aspirations.

Politics of Choice

Freedom is an individual thing. It means something singular, unique, personal for each and every person. The Chinese students want something that is not mentioned by Marx or Margaret Thatcher. They want to say what's on their minds. The right to make their own career decisions. The right to choose their college major. The right to be silly and have fun. The right to kiss your boyfriend in public. The right to mug in front of a television camera. The right to flaunt their own personal lies, concoctions, invented truths in competition with the old official lies.

Gorbachev was dismayed to find that many Soviet youth, given freedom of the press, were more interested in UFOs, punk rock, astrology, and hashish than in political issues.

Designer Memes

Most young people in the liberated lands want to de-politicize, demili-tarize, decentral-ize, secularize, and globalize.

The new breed is jumping the gene pools, form-ing post-industri-

The pop term "turn on" carries the fascinating cybernetic implication that one can selectively dial up or access brain sectors that process specific channels of information signals normally unavailable.

al, global meme-pools. They are the informates. From their earliest years, most of their defining memes came flashing at light speed across borders in digital-electronic form, light signals received by screens and radios and record players. Their habitat is the electron sphere, the environment of digital signals that is called the info world. The global village.

They are the first generation of our species to discover and explore Cyberia. They are migrating not to a new place, but to a wide open new time. The new breed is fashioning, conceiving, and designing the realities we will inhabit.

Designer Societies of the 21st Century

Who controls the screen controls the mind of the screen watcher. The power-control struggles of the early 21st Century will occur on screens in the living rooms of individuals.

In nations where religious or partisan political groups control the screens to fabricate paranoias, the people will be incited to fear, anger, and moral outrage. At the dawn of the 21st Century, the Islamic states and the USA under Republican administration effectively made this point.

The manufacture and distribution of inexpensive communications appliances and software is of enormous importance. Just as the USSR and the USA controlled the world for forty years by distributing weapons to every compliant dictatorship, Japanese and Silicon Valley companies are liberating the world with an endless flood of electronic devices designed for individuals.

The social and political implications of this democratization of the screen are enormous. In the past, friendship and intimate exchange were limited to local geography or occasional visits. Now you can play electronic tennis with a pro in Tokyo, interact with a classroom in Paris, cyberflirt with cute guys in any four cities of your choice. A global fast-feedback language of icons and memes, facilitated by instant translation devices, smoothly eliminates the barriers of language that have been responsible for most of the war and conflict of the last centuries.

Who controls the screen controls the mind of the screen watcher.

Inexpensive appliances allow individuals to write on their screens the way Gutenberg hardware-software allowed individuals to write on pages five hundred years ago. These inexpensive digitizing and editing devices are transforming the home into a cyberstudio in which individuals design, edit, perform, and transmit memes on their screens.

Individuals clothed in cyberwear will be able to meet each other in virtual realities built for two. The world becomes a neighborhood in which a person eight thousand miles away can be "right there in your windowpane."

15

CYBER CULTURES

This impassioned rhetoric was the first time that the leader of a superpower or empire had ever used the powerful meme: "generation." J.F.K. was a memetic agent, literally creating a new breed!

Did the speech writers who in 1960 passed along to Jack Kennedy that famous "torch" quote intuit what was going to happen? Did they foresee that the next two decades would produce, for the first time in human history, an economic, political power base called "the youth culture"?

In the Fifties, this new baby-boom generation was tuning in the dials of a new electronic-reality appliance called television to Leave It to Beaver and American Bandstand. And they were being lovingly guarded in maximum-security homes by devoted parents who had dutifully memorized Dr. Benjamin Spock's *Common-Sense Guide to Child Care.*

The basic theme of Spock's manual—we parents actually called it the Bible—is: treat your children as individuals.

This innocent bombshell exploded at a pregnant moment of postwar national prosperity and global self-confidence, The Marshall Plan was pouring billions into the rehabilitation-recovery of former enemies. Instead of looting, raping, and occupying the defeated enemies, we treated them like errant offspring who had become delinquent gang members. We helped them get on their feet again and gain self-respect. We postwar Spock parents became the first generation to honor and respect our children and to support their independence from us.

The importance of this event is hard to overestimate. The baby-boomers became the first generation of electronic consumers. Before they were ten, their brains were processing more "realities per day" than their grandparents had confronted in a year.

Parental Home Media

In 1950, the humble black-and-white television set marked the birth of the electronic culture. Suddenly, humans had developed electronic technology and the know-how to operate the brain and reprogram the mind.

The neurological situation is this: The language circuits of the brain are imprinted between ages three and eight. The media used in the home will format the brain of these children. Linguist-psychologists, like Noman Chomsky, and Piaget, demonstrated that languages are imprinted during this brief window of imprint vulnerability. This means that the home media used by the family formats the thought-process-

> **The language circuits of the brain are imprinted between ages three and eight. The media used in the home will format the brain of these children…. If the parents do not read and if there are no newspapers, magazines, or books in the house, the kids are at a tremendous disadvantage.**

ing files—left-brain mind—of the children. Mind-change—reformatting—could occur only under conditions that duplicate "the home culture."

If the parents do not read and if there are no newspapers, magazines, or books in the house, the kids are at a tremendous disadvantage when they timidly walk—or swagger—into the scary, impersonal first grade classroom. Most good teachers understand this principle, and convert the schoolroom into a homey, supportive environment.

We also sense the implications for reformatting mind-files—formerly known as remedial reading. Cultures or individuals who wish to change must use different language media. For the illiterate, delinquent gang member, we offer a maximum-security, homelike environment jammed with media coaches. Malcolm X, for example, was taught to read by a stern, loving parent figure in a Massachusetts prison.

And the rest you oughta know!

Stages of Humanization

As I flash back on my seventy-six years of service as Self-Appointed Change Agent and Evolutionary Scout, this viewpoint comes into focus. Our species has, in seven decades, surfed bigger, faster, more complex waves of brain change than our species experienced during the last 25,000 years.

Number of tribal generations from cave-wall painting to hand-writing and large-scale, public Egyptian art (3200 B.C.)? ➾ About 1,500.

Number of feudal generations from the pyramids to Notre Dame Cathedral, oil painting, and book literacy? ➾ About 320.

Number of generations from first factory-printed book—the first home media—to the radios, telephones, record players, movies of A.D. 1950? ➾ About 23

Number of generations from passive, black-and-white television in 1950 to multi-channel, multimedia, interactive digital home-screen design? ➾ 3

If you change the language, you change the society.

Generational Thing

Each generation since 1950 is the equivalent of an age or an epic or an era in past history. Each succeeding generation has accessed more-powerful electronic-language tools. For the first time, we can understand the mechanics of evolution the language and technology. Finally, the evolution of human brain power is reaching the optimum mutation rate. Electronic brain tools change so rapidly that every fifteen to twenty years the new generation creates a new breed.

Each stage of human culture defines memetic evolution in terms of its media, its language. And the media and languages of cultures determine whether they actively evolve or if they remain passive and unchanging.

Static cultures have built-in, iron-clad linguistic protections against change. Their media-languages self-replicate via repetition, rote-learning, etc. Their reproductive media.

Languages glorify death as the step to eternal life in well-advertised, perfectly run retirement communities called Heaven, etc. Their media-languages prevent them from being exposed to, infected by, or fertilized by other languages.

In seven decades, humans surfed bigger, faster, more complex waves of brain change than our species experienced during the last 25,000 years.

To illustrate the importance of language in cultural solidarity, we cite the case of the Iranian Shi'ite ayatollahs who put a $5 million price "on the head" of author Salman Rushdie for a few taboo words in a novel published in far away England. Or the case of militant Christians who try to force tax supported schools to teach biblical creationism.

Cultures Evolve Only When Their Media Languages Have Built-In Programs:

1. To discourage rote self-replication;

2. To stimulate self-change via shock-humor, irreverent counterculture, chaotics, etc.;

3. To invite fusion with other cultures, and fusion with other media-languages.

Feudal languages gave no words or graphics that encouraged, tolerated, or even mentioned the notion of evolution during earthly life. The almighty male God creates and controls. Heaven is the destination. Chaos, complexity, change are demonized, tabooed.

Inexpensive appliances will allow individuals to write on their screens the way Gutenberg hardware–software allowed individuals to write on pages five hundred years ago.

The tech-mech engineers of the industrial age—1500-1950—published texts, manuals, and handbooks defining evolution in terms of a Newtonian-Darwinian-Gordon Liddy competitive power struggle: survival of the most brutal, and by the book.

The Information Age

In the information age, evolution is defined in terms of brain power.

- The ability to operate the brain: activate, boot up, turn on, access neuro-channels.

- The ability to reformat and re-edit mind-files.

- The ability to receive, process, send messages at light speed.

- The ability to communicate in the multimedia mode; to invent audio-graphic dictionaries and audiographic grammars.

The mainstream home-media array of inexpensive multimedia appliances has combined the computer, television, video-cassette recorder, fax, compact-disc player, telephone, etc., into one personal home-digital system. During the feudal culture, brain power changed little from century to century. In the mechanical culture, media machines like telephone and radio reached Main Street homes a few decades after their inven-

The post-political information society, which we are now developing, does not operate on the basis of obedience and conformity to dogma. It is based on individual thinking, scientific know-how, quick exchange of facts around feedback networks, high-tech ingenuity, and practical, front-line creativity. The society of the future no longer grudgingly tolerates a few open-minded innovators. The cybernetic society is totally dependent on a large pool of such people, communicating at light speed with each other across state lines and national boundaries.

tion. But the explosion of brain power in the electronic culture in the second half of the 20th Century requires precise birth dates for each generation.

Light Cultures and Countercultures

As brain power accelerates exponentially, we can locate with precision the birth dates of the post-mech cultures.

Americans who were ages three to eight around 1950 became the first primitive electronic culture. As kids, they sat in front of the television and learned how to turn on, tune in, and turn off. Let us call them the "Ike-Knows-Best-Leave-It-to-Beavers," whose parents were sometimes known by the term "conformist."

They were happy. But they were not hip. Their bland passivity instigated the perfect antidote—the counterculture, which initially appears during the sociosexual imprint window known as adolescence.

The Beats! Hipsters! Rebels! They smoked weed and scored junk. They despised television. They were shockingly literate. They wrote breakthrough poetry and poetic prose, honored jazz by ultra hip African Americans. They were sexually experimental.

It is useful to see that the beats were older than the Beavers. In the Forties, when the beats were three to eight years old, their home media were radio, films, records, books. The baby-boomers—76 million strong—were the television-watching Beavers of the Fifties and evolved into the hippies of the Sixties. Affluent, self-confident, spoiled consumers, ready to use their television radio skills to be imprinted by turning on Bob Dylan, timing in the Beatles, turning off parent songs, and fine-tuning color screens.

The Nintendo generation of the Eighties became a pioneer group of cybernauts. They were the first humans to zap through the Alice Window and change electronic patterns on the other side of the screen. They will operate in cyberspace, the electronic environment of the 21st Century.

Coming Chaos

The next couple of decades will accelerate this dizzy explosion of brain power. The fragmenting remnants of the old centralized social systems of the feudal and industrial civilizations are crumbling down.

The 21st Century will witness a new global culture, peopled by new breeds who honor human individuality, human complexity, and human potential, enlightened immortals who communicate at light speed and design the technologies for their scientific re-animation.

16

FUTURE LOOK

If one were asked to predict the next stage
of human evolution, practical common sense
suggests selecting the identifying survival characteristic of our species, what are our survival
assets?

The instant glib answer would be that our
species is defined by our enormous brains. Our
survival asset is not hive intelligence, as in the
social insects, but individual intelligence. Our
species is classified as *Homo sapiens sapiens.*
Victorian scholars apparently decided that we
are the creatures who "think about thinking."
Our growth as a species centers on our ability to
think and communicate. Predictions about our
future would focus on improvements in the way
we think

Our young, rookie species has recently passed
through several stages of intelligence:

1. Tribal: For at least 22,000 years—approximately 25,000 to 3000 B.C.—the technolo-

gies for sapient thinking—communicating were those of a five year old child: bodily, i.e., oral-gestural.

2. Feudal: During an exciting period of approximately 3,350 years—3000 B.C. to A.D. 350—humans living north of the 35th-parallel latitude developed organized feudal agricultural societies. The technologies for thinking-communicating were hand-tooled statues, temples, monuments. Their philosophy was enforced by emperors, caliphs, and kings.

3. It took approximately 1,250 years—A.D. 350 to 1600—to co-opt the feudal kings and to establish the mechanical assembly-line managerial society. In this age, the technologies of thought communication were mechanical printing presses, typewriters, telephones, produced by efficient workers in highly organized factories, run by centralized bureaucracies.

These days most people in the industrial sectors are extremely dependent on digital thoughts and light images presented on screens. The average American

The baby-boomers were the first generation of electronic consumers. Before they were ten, their brains were processing more "realities per day" than their grandparents had confronted in a year.

household watches television 7.4 hours a day. Almost all business transactions are run by software programs communicated on screens. Without conscious choice or fanfare we have migrated from the "real worlds" of voice, hand, machine into the digitized info-worlds variously called hyperspace, cyberspace, or digital physics.

This migration across the screen into the digital info-world marks the first phase of the postindustrial society.

By the end of the first decade in the 21st Century, most humans living in post-industrial habitats will be spending as much time "jacked in" to info-worlds on the other side of the screen as they spend in the material worlds. We will spend seven hours a day actively navigating, exploring, colonizing, exploiting the oceans and continents of digital data. Interscreening—creating mutual digital-realities—will be the most popular and growthful form of human communication.

Interscreening does not imply a derogation or neglect of flesh interactions. Intimacy at the digital level programs and enriches exchanges in the warm levels. You do not lessen the richness of your murmur-touch-contact with your lover because you can also communicate by phone, fax, and hand-scrawled notes. Warm-breath interactions with your touch friends will be more elegant and pleasant with the digital-reality option added.

Interscreening does not imply a derogation or neglect of flesh interactions. Intimacy at the digital level programs and enriches exchanges in the warm levels. You do not lessen the richness of your murmur-touch-contact with your lover because you can also communicate by phone, fax, and hand-scrawled notes. Warm-breath interactions with your touch friends will be more elegant and pleasant with the digital-reality option added.

Future Global Business Will Take Two Directions

➛ Cybernetic—management of the left
  brain: Mapping and colonizing the
  digital data-worlds located on the
  other side of screens. Interpersonal
  computing. Interscreening with others.
  Building communal info-structures.
  Protecting cyber-spaces from invasion
  and exploitation by others.

➛ Psybernetic—management of the right
  brain: Mapping and colonizing the
  next frontier—one's own brain. Constructing info environments in one's
  own neuroworld. Linking one's neu-
  rospace to others. Marketing, leasing,
  sharing one's brain power with others.
  Protecting one's brain from invasion
  and exploitation from without.

Digital business will be run by multinational
corporations based in Japan and Switzerland. The
"multinates" will use individual brains as tools.
Just as slaves, serfs, and prostitutes were forced to
lease their bodies during the three predigital stages, people in the early 21st Century will be leasing
their brains. Work will hardly exist. Most physical
tasks will be performed by automated machines.
Body work will be considered a primitive form of
slavery. No human will be forced by economic-po-
litical pressure to perform muscular-mechanical
tasks that can be done better by robots.

In the 21st Century, the old Judo-Christian-Moslem sects will still be around, but they will have little power beyond entertainment and amusement. The future global religion will be intelligence increase. Upgrading rpms. The two main functions of a human being are consumption and production of thought. Our genetic assignment is the receiving, processing, and producing of digital information.

If you think like a bureaucrat,

a functionary, a manager, an

unquestioning member of a large

organization, or a chess player,

beware:

You may soon be
out-thought!

The Personal Computer was
invented by two bearded,
long-haired guys, St. Stephen
the Greater and St. Steven the
Lesser. And to complete the
biblical metaphor, the infant
prodigy was named after the
Fruit of the Tree of Knowledge:
the Apple! The controlled substance with which Eve committed the first original sin:
Thinking for Herself!

17

A CYBERPUNK MANIFESTO

by Christian A. Kirtchev

We are the **Electronic Minds**, a group of free-minded rebels. Cyberpunks. We live in Cyberspace, we are everywhere, we know no boundaries. This is our manifest. The Cyberpunks' manifest.

I. Cyberpunk

1. We are those, the Different. Technological rats, swimming in the ocean of information.

2. We are the retiring, little kid at school, sitting at the last desk, in the corner of the class room.

3. We are the teenager everybody considers strange.

4. We are the student hacking computer systems, exploring the depth of his reach.

5. We are the grown-up in the park, sitting on a bench, laptop on his knees, programming the last virtual reality.

6. Ours is the garage, stuffed with electronics. The soldering iron in the corner of the desk and the nearby disassembled radio—they are also ours. Ours is the cellar with computers, buzzing printers and beeping modems.

7. We are those who see reality in a different way. Our point of view shows more than ordinary people can see. They see only what is outside, but we see what is inside. That's what we are—realists with the glasses of dreamers.

8. We are those strange people, almost unknown to the neighborhood. People, indulged in their own thoughts, sitting day after day before the computer, ransacking the net for something. We are not often out of home, just from time to time, only to go to the nearby radio shack, or to the usual bar to meet some of the few friends we have, or to meet a client, or to the backstreet druggist—or just for a little walk.

9. We do not have many friends, only a few with whom we go to parties. Everybody else we know we know on the net. Our real friends are there, on the other side of the line. We know them from our favorite IRC channel, from the News-Groups, from the systems we hang-around.

10. We are those who don't give a shit about what people think about us, we don't care what we look like or what people say about us in our absence.

11. The majority of us like to live in hiding, being unknown to everybody except those few we must inevitably have contact with.

12. Others love publicity, they love fame. They are all known in the underground world. Their names are often heard there. But we are all united by one thing—we are Cyberpunks.

13. Society does not understand us, we are "weird" and "crazy" people in the eyes of the ordinary people who live far from information and free ideas. Society denies our way of thinking—a society, living, thinking and breathing in one and only one way—a cliché.

14. They deny us for we think like free people, and free thinking is forbidden.

15. The Cyberpunk has outer appearance, he is no motion. Cyberpunks are people, starting from the ordinary and known to nobody person, to the artist-technomaniac, to the musician, playing electronic music, to the superficial scholar.

16. The Cyberpunk is no literature genre anymore, not even an ordinary subculture. The Cyberpunk is a stand-alone new culture, offspring of the new age. A culture that unites our common interests and views. We are a unit. We are Cyberpunks.

II. Society

1. The Society which surrounds us is clogged with conservancy pulling everything and everybody to itself, while it sinks slowly in the quicksands of time.

2. However doggedly some refuse to believe it, it is obvious that we live in a sick society. The so-called reforms which our governments so adeptly use to boast, are nothing else but a little step forward, when a whole jump can be done.

3. People fear the new and unknown. They prefer the old, the known and checked truths. They are afraid of what the new can bring to them. They are afraid that they can lose what they have.

4. Their fear is so strong that it has pro-
   claimed the revolutionary a foe and the free
   idea—its weapon. That's their fault.

5. People must leave this fear behind and go
   ahead. What's the sense to stick to the little
   you have now when you can have more tomorrow. Everything they must do is stretch
   their hands and feel for the new; give freedom to thoughts, ideas, to words.

6. For centuries each generation has been
   brought up in a same pattern. Ideals is
   what everybody follows. Individuality is
   forgotten. People think in a same way, following the cliché drilled in them in child-
   hood, the cliché-education for all children.
   And, when someone dares defy authority,
   he is punished and given as a bad example.
   "Here is what happens to you when you
   express your own opinion and deny your
   teacher's one".

7. Our society is sick and needs to be healed.
   The cure is a change in the system....

III. The System

1. The System. Centuries-old, existing on principles that hang no more today. A System that
   has not changed much since the day of its birth.

2. The System is wrong.

3. The System must impose its truth upon us
   so that it can rule. The government needs
   us to follow it blindly. For this reason we
   live in an informational eclipse. When
   people acquire information other than that
   from the government, they cannot distinguish the right from the wrong. So the lie
   becomes a truth—a truth, fundamental to
   everything else. Thus the leaders control
   with lies and the ordinary people have no

notion of what is true and follow the government blindly, trusting it.

4. We fight for freedom of information. We fight for freedom of speech and press. For the freedom to express our thoughts freely, without being persecuted by the System.

5. Even in the most-developed and 'democratic' countries, the system imposes misinformation. Even in the countries that pretend to be the cradle of free speech. Misinformation is one of the System's main weapons. A weapon, they use very well.

6. It is the Net that helps us spread the information freely. The Net, with no boundaries and information limit.

7. Ours is yours; yours is ours.

8. Everyone can share information; no restrictions.

9. Encrypting of information is our weapon. Thus the words of revolution can spread uninterrupted, and the government can only guess.

10. The Net is our realm. In the Net we are Kings

11. Laws. The world is changing, but the laws remain the same. The System is not changing, only a few details get redressed for the new time, but everything in the concept remains the same.

12. We need new laws. Laws, fitting the times we live in, with the world that surrounds us. Not laws build on the basis of the past. Laws, build for today, laws that will fit tomorrow.

13. The laws that only refrain us. Laws that badly need revision.

IV. The Vision

1. Some people do not care much about what happens globally. They care about what happens around them, in their micro-universe.

2. These people can only see a dark future, for they can only see the life they live now.

3. Others show some concern about the global affairs. They are interested in everything, in the future in perspective, in what is going to happen globally.

4. They have a more optimistic view. To them the future is cleaner and more beautiful, for they can see into it and they see a more mature man, a wiser world.

5. We are in the middle. We are interested in what happens now, and in what's gonna happen tomorrow as well.

6. We look in the Net, and the Net is growing wide and wider.

7. Soon everything in this world will be swallowed by the Net: from the military systems to the PC at home.

8. But the Net is a house of anarchy.

9. It cannot be controlled and in this is its power.

10. Every man will be dependent on the Net.

11. The whole information will be there, locked in the abysses of zeros and ones.

12. Who controls the Net, controls the information.

13. We will live in a mixture of past and present.

14. The bad come from the man, and the good comes from technology.

15. The Net will control the little man, and we will control the Net.

16. For if you do not control, you will be controlled.

17. The Information is POWER!

V. Where are we?

1. Where are we?

2. We all live in a sick world, where hatred is a weapon, and freedom—a dream.

3. The world grows so slowly. It is hard for a Cyberpunk to live in an underdeveloped world, looking at the people around him, seeing how wrongly they develop.

4. We go ahead, they pull us back again. Society suppresses us. Yes, it suppresses the freedom of thought. With its cruel education programs in schools and universities. They drill in the children their view of things and every attempt to express a different opinion is denied and punished.

5. Our kids grow educated in this old and still unchanged System. A System that tolerates no freedom of thought and demands a strict obeyance to the rules.

6. In what a world, how different from this, could we live now, if people were making jumps and not creeps.

7. It is so hard to live in this world, Cyberpunk.

8. It is as if time has stopped.

9. We live on the right spot, but not in the right time.

10. Everything is so ordinary, people are all the same, their deeds too. As if society feels an urgent need to live back in time.

11. Some, trying to find their own world, the world of a Cyberpunk, and finding it, build their own world. Build in their thoughts, it changes reality, lays over it and thus they live in a virtual world. The thought-up, build upon reality.

12. Others simply get accustomed to the world as it is. They continue to live in it, although they dislike it. They have no other choice but the bare hope that the world will go out of its hollow and will go ahead.

13. What we are trying to do is change the situation. We are trying to adjust the present world to our needs and views. To use maximally what is fit and to ignore the trash. Where we can't, we just live in this world, like Cyberpunks, no matter how hard, when society fights us we fight back.

14. We build our worlds in Cyberspace.

15. Among the zeros and ones, among the bits of information.

16. We build our community. The community of Cyberpunks.

Unite!

Fight for your rights!

Christian A. Kirtchev is Kristiyan's pen name.

Kristiyan Kirchev
A Cyberpunk Manifesto

Born in Eastern Europe, **Kristiyan Kirchev** grew up in the uncertainty of fallen communism and the exciting emerge of networked computer technologies.

Trained as a carpenter, Kristiyan mastered his cyber competencies hacking his way through the wild electronic frontier, while traveling the seas onboard a cargo ship.

Along with *A Cyberpunk Manifesto* Kristiyan has authored sci-fi stories in electronic 'zines and articles in media ecology, avatar fashion, and cybermind navigation. In Kristiyan's view the computer networks are only natural element of the evolution where the mind just like the computer serves as a tool in the transition to a greater existence, which in the future would be hardware independent, i.e. telepathy without phone and "knowing" without Googling. A couple of Kristiyan's on-line works, such as the "Desktop Exhibitions" posted in a Bulgarian web media, was juggling with issues such as computer screen desktop wallpapers replacing the actual paintings at home, and using the software icon as a paintbrush of expression in the boring office life.

kristiyan@gmail.com; http://k.cult.bg

Our genetic assignment is the receiving, processing, and producing of digital information.

Ronin Books for Independent

THE FIGUTIVE PHILOSOPHER..Leary/FIGPHI $12.95 ___
From Harvard Professor to fugitive—the amazing story.

PSYCHEDELIC PRAYERS...Leary/PSYPRA $12.95 ___
Guide to transcendental experience based on Tao Te Ching

PSYCHEDELIC PRAYERS—Keepsake Edition...........................Leary $20.00 ___
Hard cover—makes a great gift for 60s enthusiast

HIGH PRIEST..Leary/HIGPRI $19.95 ___
Acid trips lead by Huxley, Ginsburg, Burroughs, Ram Dass and other 60s gurus

HIGH PRIEST—Collector's Edition...Leary $100.00 ___
Limited edition in hard cover, numbered and signed by Timothy Leary

POLITICS OF ECSTASY.....................................Leary/POLECS $14.95 ___
Classic, the book that got Leary called the "most dangerous man in America"

CHANGE YOUR BRAIN...LearyCHAYOU $12.95 ___
Brain change is more taboo than sex and why

DISCORDIA...DISCORD $14.00 ___
Parody of religion based upon Eris, goddess of chaos & confusion.

EVOULTIONARY AGENTS:...Leary/EVOAGE $12.95 ___
Leary's future history. Why the only smart thing to do is to get smarter.

POLITICS OF SELF-DETERMINATION......................Leary/POLSEL $12.95 ___
Leary's pre-Harvard years & his *real* claim to fame that got him to Harvard.

MUSINGS ON HUMAN METAMORPHOSES ....Leary/MUSING $12.95 ___
Spin psychology. Mutants and malcontents migrate first. The only place to go is up!

THE WAY OF THE RONIN...Potter/WAYRON $14.95 ___
Maverick career strategy for riding the waves of chaos at work.

POLITICS OF PSYCHOPHARMOCOLOGY.................Leary/POLPSY $12.95 ___
Story of Tim's persecution for his ideas including interrogation by Teddy Kennedy.

CHAOS AND CYBER CULTURE................................Leary/CHACYB $29.95 ___
Cyberpunk manifesto on designing chaos and fashioning personal disorders

START YOUR OWN RELIGION.................................. Leary/STAREL $14.00 ___
Gather your cult, write your own New Testiment, select your sacrament.

Books prices: **SUBTOTAL** $_____

CA customers add sales tax 8.75% _____

BASIC SHIPPING: (All orders) **$6.00**

PLUS SHIPPING: USA+$1/bk, Canada+$2/bk, Europe+$6/bk, Pacific+$8/bk _____

Books + Tax + Basic shipping + Shipping per book: TOTAL $_____

Check/MO payable to **Ronin Publishing**

MC __ Visa __ Discover __ Exp date _ _ / _ _ card #:____/____/____/____

Signature _____

Ronin Publishing, Inc • Box 22900 • Oakland, CA 94609
Ph:800/858.2665 • Fax:510/420-3672
www.roninpub.com for online catalog
Price & availability subject to change without notice

Reboot Your Brain Change Reality Screens